The MASTIFF

By Marie Antoinette Moore

Arranged and Edited by
William W. Denlinger and R. Annabel Rathman

Cover design by
Bruce Parker

DENLINGER'S PUBLISHERS, LTD.
Box 76, Fairfax, Virginia 22030

English and American Ch. Rhinehart of Blackroc (1960-1967), owned by Mooreleigh Kennels.

THIS BOOK IS DEDICATED TO:
ENGLISH AND AMERICAN CHAMPION
"RHINEHART OF BLACKROC"
HE WAS MY FRIEND . . .

International Standard Book Number: 0-87714-059-6

Library of Congress Catalog Card Number: 77-087765

Preface

The character, sensibilities, and intellectual faculties of animals have always been a favorite study and they are, perhaps, more strongly developed in the dog than in any other quadruped, from the circumstance of his being the constant companion of man. I am aware of how much has been written on this subject, but having accumulated much interesting material pertaining to the Mastiff breed, I have in this work tried to gather together all of the relevant information, both real and fictional, that I could find. My sincere thanks go to the many friends who have been helpful to me.

This is a pleasing task, arising from the conviction that the more the character of the dog is known, the better his treatment will be and the stronger the sympathy excited in his behalf.

Let me hope that the examples which are given in the following pages will help to produce this effect, and that the friend so faithful, a protector so disinterested and courageous, will meet with that kindness and affection he so well deserves.

M.A.M.

Silver statue of Ch. Bailint of Havengore belonging to Mr. and Mrs. Ivan Monostori, Oxford, England.

Hillcrest Sir Black Mask, owned by Mr. and Mrs. Harmon B. Miller.

Contents

Reproduced on the front cover of this book is a painting by Bridgit Olensharen of English and American Ch. Rhinehart of Blackroc. On the back cover is a reproduction of a photograph of the engraved glass goblet presented to Mrs. Norah Dickin (Goring Kennels, England) by members of the Old English Mastiff Club in appreciation for her many years of service to the breed and the Club.

English and American Ch. Falcon of Blackroc, owned by Mooreleigh Kennels.

Peter Piper, owned by M. J. Royle, Manchester, England.
From a lithograph which was published in France in 1897 and
which had originally appeared in the English *Our Dogs*.

Chapter One

History of the Mastiff

In one of the earliest books in my library, Thomas Bewick's *General History of Quadrupeds*, dated 1790, we find the following description:

"The Mastiff is much larger and stronger than the Bulldog, and seems every way formed for the important trust of guarding and securing the valuable property committed to his care. Houses, gardens, yards etc. are safe from depredations whilst in his custody. Confined during the day, as soon as the gates are locked, he is left to range at full liberty. He then goes round the premises, examines every part of them, and by loud barkings gives notice he is ready to defend his charge. Dr. Caius, in his curious treatise on British Dogs, tells us that three of these animals were reckoned a match for a bear and four for a lion."

We have an account, recorded in Stow's Annals, of an engagement between three Mastiffs and a Lion, in the presence of James the First. "One of the Dogs being put into the den, was soon disabled by the Lion; which took it by the head and neck and dragged it about. Another Dog was then let loose and served in the same manner; but the third being put in, immediately seized the Lion by the lip and held him for a considerable time; til being severely torn by his claws, the Dog was obliged to quit its hold; and the Lion, greatly exhausted in the conflict, refused to renew the engagement; but taking a sudden leap over the Dogs, fled into the interior part of his den. Two of the Dogs died of their wounds. The last survived and was taken great care of by the King's son, who said: 'He that had fought with the King of beasts should never after fight with any inferior creature.'

"The Mastiffs of Great Britain were noted in the time of the Roman Emperors; who appointed an officer, whose business it was to breed, and send from hence, such as would prove equal to the combats of the Amphitheatre.

"There are varieties of this animal, some of which are produced by a mixture with the Bull Dog. The Ban-Dog is lighter, smaller, more active and less powerful than the Mastiff, its nose is smaller and finer and its hair rougher. It is, notwithstanding, very fierce and employed in the same useful purposes as the Mastiff."

The following is adapted from the fourth edition of *The Dogs of the British Islands*, by "Stonehenge," 1882:

"Like the bulldog, the Old English Mastiff was bred in this country in the earliest times of which we have any reliable record; but, whether in these former ages the two breeds were distinctly separate, and whether the modern bulldog and Mastiff can be traced to one or the other of them, are points which must ever remain unsettled. Mr. F. Adcock and Mr. Kingdon would no doubt write half a dozen volumes in support of the antiquity and purity of their respective proteges; but after all, a jury empanelled to deliver a verdict between them would probably be discharged without agreement upon it, and I shall not certainly attempt to do that which I think a 12-man engine would fail in doing. My object is simply to describe the mastiff as I find him; but, nevertheless, I shall not refuse to lay before my readers Mr. Kingdon's views of the origin of the pure breed, which he believes to be now confined to Lyme Hall in Cheshire, and his own kennels, but most of his dogs are now more or less crossed with the modern Mastiff. He says: 'There appear to be recorded only four ancient seats of the Mastiff in its purity, and these four most celebrated strains have been preserved, each in its integrity; the oldest of these, pre-eminent for its antiquity and purity, has been thus preserved by the ancient family of Legh, at Lyme Hall in Cheshire, where it seems to have been even previous to 1415, and has been handed down by them in its integrity and purity; another at Chatsworth, by the Duke of Devonshire; a third at Elvaston Castle, by Lord Harrington; and a fourth at Hadzor Hall, by the Galtons.' Two of these four are said to be extinct, and, as he says, 'there remains only the Lyme Hall and Elvaston breeds in their legitimacy, and of these the Lyme Hall stands pre-eminent.' But, unfortunately, although it is readily admitted that a breed of Mastiffs has been maintained at Lyme Hall for many generations, there is no written evidence that it has been kept pure, and we may just as well depend on the purity of Mr. Lukey's brindled bitch with which he started his kennel, and which was bred by the Duke of Devonshire, as on that of the Lyme Hall strain. The fact really is, that there is no breed among existing British dogs which can be traced through all its generations for 200 years; and very few individuals for half that time. Foxhound and Greyhound pedigrees are the oldest and most carefully kept, but with very few exceptions even they do not extend much beyond the later period; and excluding them no breed goes back even for half a century without a doubtful link in the chain of pedigrees.

"In determining the points which are desired in any individual of a particular breed, it is idle to go back for centuries and select some strain of which we have no reliable record, and which, if obtained, would probably prove to be very different from what we want. For example, the Foxhound is said to be descended from a hound which was very different from him in many important respects; yet, according to Mr. Kingdon, we ought to take the old type and reject the modern one. Instead of proceeding in this illogical way, the Master of Hounds nowadays improves upon the old type by every possible means, and the result is a hound which does what is asked from him, in a manner which would be far beyond the powers of his ancestors. So with the Mastiff. We want a large and handsome dog, possessed of a temperament which will bear restraint under provocation, and, at the same time, of courage to defend his master till the death. These mental properties were carefully attended to by Mr. Lukey, who may be considered to be the founder of the modern English Mastiff, and his example has been carefully followed in this respect by Mr. E. Hanbury, Capt. Garnier, Miss Aglionby, Miss Hales, Mr. M. B. Wynn, Mr. Lindoe, Mr. Nichols, and Mr. W. George. All these eminent breeders have taken Mr. Lukey's breed as typical of what they desire to produce, and the results of their efforts may be compared with Mr. Kingdon's dogs on perfectly equal terms, inasmuch as it is admitted that full attention has been paid to the demand for a mild temperament and other mental attributes which are peculiarly essential to this breed."

In the first edition of *The Dogs of the British Isles* (1872), "Stonehenge" includes the following, which he quotes from a letter from Captain Garnier:

"The mighty dogs which used to be kept at Chatsworth were pure Alpine mastiffs, as also were the magnificent animals I have mentioned as having seen at Bill George's kennels some sixteen years ago; while others that I frequently used to meet with at that time were of the same character. These, one and all, presented the same type—a strong proof of their purity—and that type was in all respects the same as the old English mastiff portrayed by Vandyke. The same may be said of the dogs in Landseer's picture of Alpine mastiffs, which have all the points of the true mastiffs, although their tails, as might be expected from the cold climate, are hairier than they should be. At that time one used to meet with good English mastiffs also, but they were few compared to the number of half-bred animals that went by that name; and, with the exception of Mr. Lukey's breed, the good ones have nearly all come from Lancashire, Cheshire, and the north of England generally, where some years ago they were still in considerable request for guarding the large bleaching grounds. Between these and the Alpine dogs I never could discover the slightest difference except in size—the best English dogs varying from 29 to 33 inches at the shoulder, while the Alpine male specimens were seldom under 32 inches.

"Now it is ridiculous to suppose that the dogs that used to be found at the convent, and in a few of the Swiss valleys, were a breed indigenous to that small part of the continent of Europe; and yet it was there only that the breed existed. When, therefore, we find the same animal common in England two hundred years ago, and still to be met with in considerable numbers, though more rarely than formerly, it is only reasonable to conclude that the English and Mount St. Bernard mastiffs are identical breeds, and that the monks, requiring large, powerful, generous, and high-couraged animals for their benevolent purposes, selected the old English dog in preference to all other breeds. It is very easy to understand that with the disuse of the breed for combatting wild animals, they should have been allowed to die out and degenerate in England; and it is equally easy to understand that the mastiff kept at the Convent of St. Bernard for a particular purpose, requiring strength and courage, should have been kept up, and that the best specimens of the breed in modern times have come from there.

"The old breed can now no longer be obtained from the convent, the cause of which is thus stated by Mr. Richardson, in his valuable work on the dog, published in 1851: 'The old mastiff breed was almost completely destroyed by pestilence many years ago, and the monks were obliged to resort to a cross with the rough-coated Italian and Pyrenean wolf dogs in order to keep it up, the result being a broken-haired dog, an excellent illustration of which is to be seen in the engraving in Youatt. Since then, however, I have spoken to people who have visited the convent, and it appears that the monks have used another cross—the huge boarhounds found in Bavaria, the Upper Danube, and Tyrol.

"The points of the mastiff may be gathered from what I have already written on the subject, but for

Mastiff. Illustration by Arthur Wardle, which originally appeared in the English *Our Dogs*.

Mastiff. Illustration published by W. Darton and J. Harvey, September 1, 1808.

Mastiff Dog, by A. Bell, Sculp.

Mastiff and Greyhounds. A painting by Sawrey Gilpin, R.A., 1780, the property of Mr. E. G. Oliver.

the sake of clearness I will state them in detail. Height in dogs, originally from 31 to 34 inches at the shoulder, now from 28 to 33 inches; body long and deep, chest broad and shoulders muscular, loin broad and flat, limbs massive, with the frequent development of a fifth toe on the hind feet of the larger specimens; head above eyes very broad and full, but rounded and not square, a deep furrow down the center, and the frontal sinus much elevated; the under edge of the lower jaw deeply convex, giving it depth; muzzle broad, heavy, and blunt, but not too short; eyes small, and appearing to be deeply sunk from the loose skin of the forehead causing the eyebrows to hang over, giving the animal an expression of great sternness and dignity; ears of moderate size, and either half-erect or pendent. I have found the purest specimens with both descriptions of ear, and for my own part, somewhat prefer the half-erect, it being invariably accompanied by great nervous energy and activity. Coat originally coarse, but now, by greater domestication and perhaps also by intermixture with other breeds, much shorter and closer. Colour brindled or all shades of fallow and red, with black muzzle and ears. Brindled dogs were originally held in the highest estimation, and I have generally found them coeteris paribus, the best in other respects—the reason being doubtless that, while the lighter colour is possessed in common with some other dogs, the

brindle is the characteristic of the mastiff only, and so far is a proof of purity of the breed.

"I may remark how very few really good animals are represented at the present day."

Although these are only brief extracts from works by the aforementioned writers, I feel they do describe the scene from the latter part of the eighteenth century on into the last quarter of the nineteenth century.

The Home-Guard "Colonel." Drawn and engraved for the *American Agriculturist* by A. Bennett.

10

Coponore Junior ("Thor"), at three years of age. Owner, M. V. Tuggle, Decatur, Georgia.

Ben of Love Creek, owned by Mr. and Mrs. Lissner.

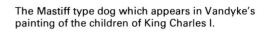
The Mastiff type dog which appears in Vandyke's painting of the children of King Charles I.

Mr. Wallace's Turk.

MR. WALLACE'S TURK.

Chapter Two

The Mastiff, by William Wade

(From *The American Book of the Dog*—1891)
(Adapted)

In writing of Mastiffs, certainly one of the very oldest breeds of dogs now existing, there is a strong temptation to go into an inquiry as to the origin of so ancient a breed; to inquire as to where it sprung from, how it was developed, etc. This, however, I cannot bring myself to do. All theories as to the matter would be but theories—everything about the question would be misty and shadowy; and where it is perfectly evident that no valid proof can be produced for any of the many theories as to the origin or relationship, of the breed, it seems to me most unprofitable to waste our time in hazardous speculations which can profit nobody.

Should there be any readers of THE AMERICAN BOOK OF THE DOG who delight in such abstruse and antiquarian pursuits, I would commend to them the admirable monograph of the Mastiff, prepared by Mr. M. B. Wynn, the noted English authority on the breed, in which work he has displayed a remarkable degree of patience, and has devoted an amount of research to this branch of the subject, demonstrating most clearly, that with him it was a labor of love.

For my part, I do not believe that the Mastiff as we have him today existed in anything but a very rough and crude form a few hundred years since. England evidently had, in a very early day, a dog used for somewhat the same purposes as the Mastiff is now used. This was "the broad-mouthed dog of Britain," but whether it was the Mastiff or the Bulldog is, to my mind, pure conjecture. Whether the Mastiff is an offshoot of the Bulldog, bred in a different direction for size, etc., or vice versa, or whether both sprung from the same root and have been differently developed, is merely guess-work, and I never had the patience to thoroughly read such tiresome gropings in the dark, except when I read Wynn as a matter of a duty.

I fancy that the earliest picture of a Mastiff, by a well-known and prominent artist, is that shown in Vandyke's picture of the children of King Charles I. As the child standing beside the dog appears to have been about twelve years old at the time, it may reasonably be assumed that the picture was painted about 1632; and that the dog shown in that picture would not be disgraced now in a class of show specimens. Mr. Wynn characterizes this dog as of Boarhound type, with which statement I cannot agree. The width of skull, the raised ridges over the eyebrows, the comparatively short muzzle, and the gentle, loving expression, are most diverse from the long muzzle, narrow skull and truculent expression common in the Boarhound. No one can study the affectionate expression of the upturned eye of the noble dog shown in this picture without experiencing a feeling of admiration for the grand character of the dog. It indicates in unmistakable terms that serious trouble would instantly befall anyone who might attempt to harm his young protégés.

Next in order of date to this picture (within my observation) comes the picture in Bingley's "Memoirs of British Quadrupeds", published in 1809, wherein a dog of admirable Mastiff type, in body and legs, is shown, but this specimen appears too much tucked in at the flanks, and with the most peculiar of heads, the muzzle being far shorter, in proportion to the general size of the dog, than in the most snub-nosed pet of the fancy of today (or rather a few years since), while the skull is preposterously long in just the same ratio that the muzzle is short.

It appears that the second type of Mastiff was a long skulled, short muzzled one. Coming on down through the Mastiff ages, we reach the picture of Lukey's Bruce 1 and 2, Lukey's Lion, Lord Waldegraves Couchez and other fountains of our present Mastiff blood, and we find dogs of what would now be called a long-faced type.

Possibly I am in error in noting these last two dogs among English Mastiffs, as both came from Mount St. Bernard; but, for all that they were of high English Mastiff type, strengthening the claim of Mr. Wynn, Colonel Garnier, and others, that the English and Alpine Mastiff only differed in point of size, the latter being the larger.

The next type illustrated is the one that would now be called houndy, a "lurcher," etc. as evidenced by the famous Old Champion Turk, Miss Hale's Lion, Colonel and Salisbury. These dogs had long muzzles, deep and blunt, showed general symmetry and vigor, and were succeeded by the "Crown Prince dispensation" of puggy, undershot muzzles, straight hocks, flabby obesity and lack of vigor. I do not mean to say that at any of these periods either type was universal; but it is certain that during the later years the rage was for certain peculiarities, and dogs not conforming to the dictates of the fashion were, in the vernacular of dog shows, "no Mastiffs". Vandyke's and Bingley's pictures only teach us that there *were* such dogs, but we do not know whether the majority of the breed then existing was of similar type; in fact, it is reasonable to assume that there was no such thing as "type" a hundred years ago. In those days, breeders bred only for specific use, and the appearance of the animal was a matter of little importance.

The early history of the Mastiff in America is a broken chapter, enveloped in a good deal of doubt. Of course Mastiffs were imported into the Colonies in early days, just as any other breed might have been, but their blood soon became mingled with that of the average dog of the land, and for years no pure strains were bred. New Englanders imported many, but, unfortunately, they were not careful as to the pedigrees they got with the animals, and the result is that "New England pedigrees" are an amusing study for their complications, and one is often puzzled to know whether the pedigree is a blundering fraud or an honest mistake.

A Mr. Lloyd Phoenix, of New York City, at an early day, imported a litter brother of the famous Champion King, and a black bitch, from the noted dealer Bill George, and there can be no doubt as to the honesty of this transaction, George being above suspicion; but, unfortunately, he preserved no records of what became of the dogs, or what offspring they left. Colonel Garnier brought a pair with him from England to Canada about 1837, which he left there on his return, taking only a son, Lion, who was afterward the sire of the noted Lukey's Governor, and considerable of this stock was scattered over this country, some going as far west as St. Louis, Mo.; but no traces can be found of them further than this. The earliest importations of stock of known breeding and high pedigree, of which any records have been kept, were those of Mr. Underwood and Mr. E. Delafield Smith of Newark, N. J., who bought some dogs from Mr. Frank Heinzman, of Bradford, England. The pedigrees of these dogs are thoroughly established and given in full, and their breeding was of the highest order. A curious mistake, however, occurred therein, in printing "Ornaker" for "Quaker." Any pedigrees running (as many do) to Delafield Smith's strain may be accepted as genuine and valuable. Mr. R. L. Belknap and Gen. S. L. M. Barlow, of New York, also imported several Mastiffs some fifteen or twenty years since; but the pedigrees of such of Mr. Belknap's as I

have seen are unsatisfactory, while those of General Barlow's Ruth and others are clear and correct.

Mr. W. H. Lee, of Boston, made an important record as a Mastiff breeder about 1883, owning Turk, a fine dog of the older type, and having imported Ilford Cromwell, Dr. J. W. Alsop, of Middletown, Conn., also did good service about the same time, importing Boadicea, by Rajah; and the Pelham Manor Kennels, by importing Cato and Queen II. Mr. Charles H. Morgan, of Worcester, Mass., imported Duchess of Connaught, and Mr. Herbert Mead, of Lake Waccabuc, N. Y., imported Princess Royal, Aydah, and Fairy.

The most decided impetus to Mastiff interests of late years was given by the starting of the Ashmont Kennels, of Boston, Mass., by Dr. J. Frank Perry, with such dogs as Hero II, Ilford Cromwell, Lorna Doone, Bal-Gal, etc., which may be said to have started the movement that led to the importation of such dogs as Ilford Caution, Minting, Alonzo, Ilford Chancellor, Lady Coleus, Lady Phyllis, Countess of Dunsmore, Ilford Comedy, Phaedra, Cambrian Princess, Beaufort, Gerda, Moses, Rosalind, Prussian Princess, Lady Gladys, etc.

The leading breeder in the country today is Mr. E. H. Moore of Melrose, Mass., with Ilford Chancellor as stud dog, and his galaxy of brood bitches includes Cambrian Princess, Lady Coleus, Lady Phyllis, Lady Margery, etc.; a collection not excelled either in England or in this country.

Certainly the Mastiff has come to stay. Other breeds of large dogs may temporarily overshadow him, in point of numbers or popular fancy, but the Mastiff has too firm a position in the canine interests of the country—he represents too much of the wealth of the canine world, and is too highly appreciated by dog-fanciers of all classes—to ever be neglected, either at home or on the show bench.

In one respect, the grand characteristics of the Mastiff have undergone little change—I might say almost none—as compared with the vast changes that have occurred in physical conformation. One of the very earliest English writers on dogs—Doctor Caius, I think—mentions "the Mastie that keepyth the house." Bingley gives the Mastiff a reputation for wise discrimination, careful watchfulness, vigilance, and fondness for affording protection, that seems an inherent characteristic of the race from its origin to the present day. I have known pets of the show ring, dogs of the bluest of blue blood, such as Lord Raglan (brother to the famous champion Orlando), Boadicea (by Rajah),

Persephone (by Debonair ex a Crown Prince bitch), the long faced, snipey Gipsey, and others of her ilk, to display the same general measure of wisdom as watch-dogs; and it is as the watch-dog *par excellence* that the Mastiff is admired. Undoubtedly dogs of other breeds, and even mongrels, often (but not generally) display the same traits that so glorify the Mastiff. For instance, I know that the Champion St. Bernard Barry was eminent in this respect; but I also know that in this respect Mastiffs average much higher than any other breed. I have owned and known, intimately, with abundant opportunity to study them, fully a hundred Mastiffs, and in that number there was but one real savage dog; but one that would attack except as a last resort.

Gipsey, Lion, Ginger, Lee's Turk, Boadicea, and Winifred all had the strong disposition to accompany members of the families when they went away from home, particularly if the person was a woman or a child. It was some trouble to coax Lion to go off the place with a man, and almost impossible to do so in daylight; but if a woman went away at night, he would use every endeavour to go with her, and if he couldn't go, would fume and fret in the most vexed manner. Gipsey would never let my four-year-old boy go off the place alone without getting up and going with him. Any of the dogs I have mentioned, when in charge of any person on a walk at night, might stray a considerable distance away from their charge; but let them hear a strange footstep, and they would

Mastiff. Dr. J. Sidney Turner's Beaufort. Sire, Mr. Mark Beaufoy's Beau, by Prince out of Belle. Dam, Dr. J. Sidney Turner's The Lady Isabel, by Crown Prince out of Lady Rowena. Engraved by A. F. Lydon and published in *British Dogs,* 1889.

Mooreleigh Maurice (1950). Bred and owned by Mooreleigh Kennels.

immediately draw near the person they were escorting, and remain near until the strange footstep was lost in the distance. These are but specimen bricks from many kilnfuls that I could deliver; and it will be noted that in no case did the Mastiff resort to violence, gentle means in each case proving sufficient.

But will a Mastiff attack, rend, and tear if occasion demands? Listen: Lion was accustomed to working-men coming around my place in their working clothes, and beyond keeping a careful watch over them and occasionally remonstrating against what he deemed improper conduct, never molested anybody; but one morning a typical tramp came to the back door—one of your regular dyed-in-the-wool, dirty, ragged, frowsy, red-faced tramps, stinking of whiskey. Just as the cook opened the door, Lion came around the side of the house, and with one short, hurried bark, sprung straight at the fellow's throat. The cook interfered and ordered the dog off, but she might as well have whistled to the wind; and when she

caught him by the collar, he jerked her across the floor as if she had been a feather, until the hired man came to her aid and succeeded in depriving Lion of a taste of that tramp. It is unnecessary to add that when my people finally got the dog under control, the tramp was out of sight, and for aught I know is running yet. Now, so obedient was Lion to that cook, under ordinary circumstances, that if she put food for him on the floor and said "Lion, don't you touch that," he would back off, lick his lips, eye the food in the most wistful manner, but would lie by it all day without touching it. He knew, however, that his duty in life was to dispose of tough-looking tramps, and no order would drive him from so relished a duty.

That this role of protector should be the Mastiff's inborn disposition is perfectly natural; as long since as the time of Queen Elizabeth he was "the Mastie that keepyth the house," and for centuries previous this must have been his vocation, to have established it so firmly as his character. After perhaps six hundred years of use for this purpose, it is not, I repeat, strange that protection of life and property should be the one object in life of this grand dog. If I have not made it sufficiently plain, let me say now that the crowning glory of the Mastiff, and the immeasurable value of the breed as watch-dogs, lie in the marked unwillingness to resort to strong measures until mild ones have been tried and failed. Almost any breed of dogs, or non-breed, will attack strangers if need be, but the Mastiff is the only dog whose special characteristic it is not to attack until warning threats have failed.

As to what a Mastiff should be in conformation, much, if not all, depends on which post you wish to tie. If you wish to win prizes at dog shows, be exalted as owning "that crack Mastiff," the nearer that you can get to the standard laid down by Mr. M. B. Wynn for the original Mastiff Club of England the better. If you interpret this standard and scale of points with strictness in every particular, and breed to it faithfully, you will get dogs that will be, bodily, at least, all you want, and it may be mentally; but if because the scale allots forty points in a hundred to head properties, you magnify that forty to ninety-nine, and condone weak loins, straight hocks, too short bodies, weak joints, and frightfully undershot muzzles, as weighing nothing against "that grand head", you will probably get waddling, ugly brutes that will never rise above the position of prize-winners under "fancy" judges. That this standard and scale of points can be carried out, and still breed

Mastiffs as the result, is shown by the grand dog Beaufort, chosen as an illustration of this article, a dog with the extreme of short face and realizing as near the ideal of the standard as a dog is likely ever to do, yet without a single deformity and not overdone in a single particular. His only fault, if fault it may be termed, are large dew-claws, which impede his action behind, and which should have been removed when a puppy, as they possess no "fancy" merit or demerit, being simply "admissible." Beaufort's merits are in his excellent fore legs, straight and strong, his deep, capacious chest, his admirable hind legs, with perfection in hocks, the very broad, flat kind most desirable in Mastiffs, his vast skull, neat ears, and bulky loin. His head is fashionable today, but should the longer head of Turk, Colonel, etc., become the fashion in years to come, Beaufort will still be thoroughly Mastiff in bodily properties.

The dog to breed to is the one noted for getting good ones, and when you strike a good strain, stick to it as long as it can be sustained. Remember that, in many cases, great show bitches are miserable failures as producers. The rules for rearing Mastiffs, as distinct from those applying to other breeds, are few and simple, but it may be especially said of them that above all other breeds they need the most abundant exercise while young. They are certainly lazy dogs, indisposed to exertion, and if reared singly are not likely to take the required amount of exercise. To supply this, it is well to procure some kind of playmate for the youngsters; any cur will answer, as long as it be playful and not too small. If reared in litters, the Mastiff puppies will stimulate each other sufficiently. Distrust a stud dog that is cooped up without free exercise; some under these circumstances do not seem to fail as stock-getters, others do. Lord Raglan was set down as impotent until his last owner put him on the road, following his buggy, then he got puppies with as much certainty as the average stud dog.

In estimating the scale of points laid down by Mr. Wynn, it must be remembered that it was framed by a fanatic on "head," one who exalted that property as high as anybody, but who at the same time insisted on bodily vigor, muscular development, and the utmost activity. I would remark as to his requirement "expression lowering," that this must not be understood as savage or sullen, but that the dog must present such an appearance as is calculated to deter trespassers, and as a corollary, he must be above permitting undue familiarity from strangers. His work is that of

Friar Tuck of Havengore (1961-1973). From a 1972 photograph. Sire, Withybush Prashna of Zimapan. Dam, Robin of Havengore. Owners, Dr. and Mrs. Dwayne L. Nash, Lodi, California.

Caesar of Seattle, C.D. Breeders, Mr. and Mrs. Stuart C. Olsen, Haywood, Virginia. Owners, Mr. and Mrs. David Cole, Seattle, Washington.

watch-dog, and such a dog must not make up with every stranger that comes along. As "an ounce of prevention is worth a pound of cure," it is best to have your watch-dog impress people that they must behave with circumspection, rather than that he should invite them into doing as they please and then have to check them.

To anyone who wishes to rear a true Mastiff, in all his perfection of utility, let me say: Begin by making a friend of your dog; let him accompany you on your walks abroad; let him come into your house and lie before your fire, and in every way connect himself with you and your welfare. If you shut him out of your house, how in the name of common sense is he to know that he has any part or interest in it? You might as well expect watching from one of a litter of black Essex pigs. Don't attempt to "conquer" him, "break him in," or any of the brutalities common to the vulgar dog-breaker; a Mastiff that can be "conquered" is not the animal you could trust were you engaged in a battle to the death with a vicious burglar or tramp; nor would such an animal be a Bayard in the protection of your wife and children in a lonely farm-house, with you far away. Grave faults, such as killing chickens, etc., must be eradicated, but don't go at it with a club. Remember how you would treat your child in such a case, and try to follow the same lines with your dog, of course allowing for the difference in mental capacity. First love your dog, next make him love you; you will never regret having gained his love and confidence, and the day may come when you will be repaid a hundred fold.

I give you the standard set forth by the original Mastiff Club of England, in preference to that prepared by the present Old English Mastiff Club, as it is simpler, being free from much technicality, and therefore more readily comprehended by a layman. In all essentials the two are substantially the same.

Mooreleigh Moonlight ("Cindy"). Owner, Robert Graham Wahn, Locust Valley, New York.

Head

General—Very massive and short, with great breadth and depth of skull, and squareness of muzzle. Expression lowering.

Forehead—Broad, flat, and wrinkled; eyebrows heavy, with a broad stop extending well into the forehead.

Cheeks—Full.

Eyes—Wide apart, small, and sunken; dark brown in color.

Muzzle—Short, truncated, deep and broad, not tapering toward the nose; jaws very wide; line of profile from stop level, not drooping toward the nose (i.e. not Hound-muzzled); black in color.

Nose—Large; nostrils large, and a well-marked line between.

Lips—Thick and pendulous; they should fall forward (not hang at the corners of the mouth as in the Bloodhound).

Teeth—Large, undershot or level.

Ears—Small, pendent or semi-erect, not placed low as in the Hound; the darker the color the better.

Body

General—Thick-set and muscular, with great length and bulk, on comparatively short legs.

Neck—Short, thick, and muscular; dewlap slightly developed.

Chest—Deep, wide between fore legs.

Shoulders—Wide apart across breast and back; shoulder-blades deep.

Back—Long and broad.

Loin—Broad, flat, and muscular.

Thighs—Straight, muscular, and thick.

Stern—Fine, short, straight, thick at root, tapering to tip, and carried generally down.

Fore legs—Short, from elbow to ground straight, with plenty of bone and muscle.

Hind legs—Straight, well curved from stifle to hock, with plenty of bone; dew-claws admissible.

Feet—Round, large, and compact.

Coat—Hard, short, and fine.

Color—Fawn with black ears and muzzle, or good brindles equal pieds are admissible and equal for purity—award no points for color.

Height

General—Produced by depth of body, not by length of limb.

Dogs—From twenty-seven inches at shoulder and upward; the greater the height the better, providing there is no loss of symmetry and character, and that the weight increase in proportion.

Bitches—Generally average three inches less than dogs.

Ch. King, whelped 1865, winner of many prizes. Sire, Lukey's Rufus. Dam, Fields "Nell." Painting by Harrison Weil, 1866.

Mrs. Harmon Miller and Hillcrest Sir Black Mask.

Mooreleigh Undine at ten months.   Owner, Gerald Danaher.

Chapter Three

The Mastiff, by Hugh Dalziel
(From British Dogs—1889) (Adapted)

The Mastiff is one of the three kinds of Cur dog mentioned in the old Welsh laws of the ninth century, and by old English writers the Mastiff is constantly referred to as a house-dog and guardian of live stock and other property.

The "Mayster of Game" writes of the Mastiff: "His office is for to kepe his maistre's beestis, and his maistre's hous, and it is a good nature of houndis for thei kepen and defenden at her power al her maistre's goodes, thei byn of cherlich nater, and of foule shap."

Barnaby Googe, in the sixteenth century, gives the following picture of the Mastiff:

The Bandog for the House.—But now I will only speak of dogs for the husbands, and keepers both of the house and the cattle: and first of the Mastie that keepeth the house: for this purpose you must provide you such a one, as hath a large and mighty body, a great and shrill voice, that both with his barking he may discover, and with his sight dismay the thief, yea being not seen, with the horror of his voice put him to flight. His stature must neither be long nor short, but well set, his head great, his eyes sharp and firey, either brown or gray, his lips blackish, neither turning up, nor hanging too much down, his mouth black and wide, his neather jaws fat, and coming out of it of either side a fang, appearing more outward than his other teeth, his upper teeth even with his neather, not hanging too much over, sharp and hidden with his lips, his countenance like a lion, his breast great and shaghaired, his shoulders broad, his legs big, his tail short, his feet very great, his disposition must neither be too gentle, nor too curst, that he may neither fawn upon a thief, nor fly upon his friends, very waking, no gadder abroad, nor lavish of his mouth, barking without cause, neither maketh it any matter though he be not swift: for he is but to fight at home, and to give warning of the enemy."

It seems clear enough that, co-extensive with the known history of these islands, a dog representing, however roughly, the modern Mastiff, has existed, and at an early date he was known in England by that name. In the forest laws of Henry II, if not earlier, the keeping of these dogs in or near royal forests was the subject of special regulations which would now be considered cruel and oppressive. The statute which prohibited all but a few privileged individuals from keeping Greyhounds or Spaniels provided that farmers and substantial freeholders, dwelling within the forests, might keep Mastiffs for the defence of their houses within the same, provided such Mastiffs be expeditated according to the laws of the forest.

This "expeditating," "hambling," or "lawing," as it was indifferently termed, was intended so to maim the dog as to reduce to a minimum the chances of his chasing and seizing the deer, and the law enforced its being done after the following manner: "Three claws of the fore foot shall be cut off by the skin, by setting one of his fore feet upon a piece of wood 8 in. thick, and 1 ft. square, and with a mallet, setting a chisel of 2 in. broad upon the three claws of his fore feet, and at one blow cutting them clean off."

This just enables us to look at the Mastiffs of that day as through a narrow chink in the wall of silence that hides from us the past. The 2 in. chisel was intended to cut the three doomed claws off at one blow; how much wider would it require to be to perform its work efficiently on some of our best specimens?—considerably so, I think, to make the "clean" job of it the instructions intended to provide for; and we may, therefore, fairly infer that the dogs were altogether less in size than the grand, massive animals that we can boast of today.

Coming down to the time of Caius and Cotgrave, who both wrote in the reign of Elizabeth, Mastiffs and Bulldogs are both mentioned, but no description of any accuracy is given of either; and to construct, from the loose references made to them, a dog sufficiently satisfying for a modern fancier, requires the active aid of imagination, which, I find, often assists writers towards what they wish may have been, facts of the slightest character being strained to support pet theories.

For my own part, I feel convinced that the Mastiff and the Bulldog have sprung from a common origin. The attributes which they still have in common, after so many years of breeding towards opposite points, strengthens me in this belief, which is still further confirmed by a study of the various engravings and paintings made of them from time to time, which I have been able to consult, all of which show that the further we go back, starting from "Stonehenge" on "The Dog," the more closely do the two breeds assimilate in general character.

Of our present dogs, the strain for which the greatest, or rather absolute, purity is claimed is the Lyme Hall Mastiff, which has been in the Legh family since the beginning of the fifteenth century, if not from a still earlier date; but whether the existing dogs of this strain have been kept pure by absolute in-and-in breeding, or with such merely occasional cross with some closely-allied strain as may have been found necessary to prevent deterioration, so that we may rely on it as representing the original type, I have no means of knowing. As it is held as a pure representative of the old English Mastiff by the family who have so long had it in their possession, I can have no doubt that good reasons for that belief exist, and that the strain is at least approximately pure, and best represents the whole breed. I am not aware that any other breeders claim anything approaching to such a long descent for their dogs, although a strain so noted as the Lyme Hall must long have been would be sure to spread and leave its mark on such other kennels as were most likely to be preserved with some degree of purity.

Of late years the champion of the Lyme Hall Mastiff has been Mr. H. D. Kingdon, of Willhayne, Devon, who obtained the breed from Lyme Hall by the courtesy of the present Mr. Legh, and who insists on their superiority over all others with a tenacity, and, I might say, dogged obstinacy, thoroughly English, and worthy of the breed he admires. I cannot say, however, that I agree with him in his absolute worship of what he calls purity; when that term is applied to dogs of any breed, my scepticism is aroused, and, indeed, even could absolute purity be proved, I would not put the high value on it that many do. Beyond a certain point, I consider this "purity" positively hurtful; I prefer, as a breeder of dogs, to look forward rather than back, and, like

> The grand old gardener and his wife,
> Smile at the claims of long descent.

The good old dogs, like the good old times, possess many advantages over the present, now that distance lends enchantment to the view; but, in my opinion, the present dogs are the best, and will as certainly be excelled by those of the future. To think otherwise would be to admit that the English, who have succeeded so unquestionably in the improvement of so many other animals, have failed with the dog.

In making these remarks, I do not disparage, nor even, I hope, under-estimate the good qualities of the Lyme Hall Mastiff. One of the most astute judges and successful breeders (Mr. Edgar Hanbury) has thought highly and written of them in most eulogistic terms, giving practical force to his expressed admiration by introducing them into his own kennels from Mr. Kingdon's; and of several of the breed that I have seen I can say they were magnificent specimens, and I regret that so few opportunities are now afforded the public of seeing them at shows, as it is only by actual comparison that a fair judgment on relative merits of animals can be formed, and in forming such judgment it is absolutely necessary for agreement that the various judges should adopt one standard of excellence.

Modern taste in Mastiffs seems to require, above all things, size and symmetry; and what I contend for is that modern taste has a perfect right to demand what it pleases in such matters. The great evil to be guarded against is variation of the standard; this should not be altered at the caprice of judges or societies—whose position gives them an adventitious influence in forming public taste and opinion—to such an extent as to change the type. Now, to put a case: if I considered it necessary to cross the Mastiff with the Boarhound in order to gain the desired size, and, having gained that point, went back to the Mastiff to eliminate other elements which the Boarhound cross had introduced, but which I did not want, I would expect that some members for a number of generations would, to use a favourite expression of Mr. Kingdon's, exhibit "the discordant elements of which their ancestors were compounded"; but I would also expect that the seventh or eighth generation at furthest would show no traces of the Boarhound, and would be as fully entitled to be called pure-bred Mastiffs as any in or out of the Stud Book. Hence, in judging Mastiffs, I do not care to consider whether they were manufactured twenty years ago or have an unspotted lineage from the Flood.

This part of the subject has, however, unwittingly drawn on my space to a greater extent than I intended it should; I will, therefore, only say further, that while I think judicious crossing in this and all breeds is not only permissible within certain limits, but a necessity of improvement, it is self-evident that, although we may produce a fine dog by a mixture of breeds, we cannot have a Mastiff unless that blood is allowed to predominate, and the older and purer it is, the sooner and better it will assert itself over the introduced blood as shown in foreign features engrafted on it, yet that specially desired features, such as increased size, may, by selection, be retained.

In general appearance the Mastiff is noble and dignified; his strength is shown in his immense bone, large, square, and well-knit frame, whilst the majesty of his carriage, his grand head, and the magnanimous expression of his countenance, bespeak consciousness of power governed by a noble and courageous nature. There are Mastiffs with sinister and scowling faces, exhibiting the ferocity of the coward and bully, but these will rarely be found to possess the grandeur of form that distinguishes the breed, and are often cross-bred. In some instances a surly and dangerous disposition will show itself in otherwise good and pure dogs, and when it does, they become a positive danger even to their owners, and a terror and a nuisance to the neighbourhood in which they may be kept. The natural disposition, however, is gentle, with an intuitive desire to afford protection, so that a well-trained Mastiff is at once the best of companions—not given to quarrel, solicitous of notice from those he serves—and proves, with his intelligence and high mettle, the best of guards for person and property.

These good qualities characterise the modern Mastiff, and show the power of man in taming down the fierce nature of the fighting dogs of Britain; for in this, as in outward form, it is impossible to doubt that the animal has been greatly modified and improved since he was mainly kept in order to display his prowess in the bull-ring and the bear-garden. As to his modern uses, he is still *par excellence* the watch-dog of England, whose honest bark bays deep-mouthed welcome as we draw near home.

He is the gamekeeper's best companion and preserver from night marauders—and for this purpose a dark brindled dog is preferable to a fallow, not being so easily seen at night—and to these arduous duties have been added the lighter ones of companion to ladies and gentlemen, and the occasional display of his regal canine magnificence on the show-bench.

I have mentioned the faults of temper in dealing with the general character. I will now point out the faults in outward appearance most often met with. These are, first, I think, the ungainliness of motion caused by weak legs, particularly shown in the knee-joints and the development of cow-hocks; with this there are generally flat, lean, wasted hams, and sometimes light, weak loins, and all these, or the cow-hocks alone, give a shambling gait that is most objectionable. These defects are often caused by bad rearing, inferior or insufficient food, or want of room or dampness in the kennel. The faults alluded to are very common, and it should be the endeavour of breeders, and also of judges, to get rid of them—the latter by refusing prizes to all dogs that show the faults, and the former by judicious selection and careful rearing.

In recent years, a desire for immense bulk seems to have led exhibitors of Mastiffs to obtain this by fleshiness rather than increase of frame. This is done at a loss of symmetry and activity of action; and so over-fat are some Mastiffs when exhibited that, far from suggesting that they are a race of dogs of war, their appearance shows they would be of use only to the commissariat department of an army when besieged.

Mr. W. Wade, of Hulton, Pennsylvania, gave a prize at the English Kennel Club Show, 1887, for the Mastiff possessing the best action. The prize was won by Beaufort, and I must say, if his competitors were worse movers than he is, there is much room for improvement in that matter, which is by no means an unimportant one.

Peach Farm Michael, bred by Mrs. John F. Brill, Newark, Delaware.

Mastiff "Wolsey," the property of Mr. F. G. Banbury.

Chapter Four

The English Mastiff, by W. K. Taunton

(From *The New Book of the Dog*—1911) (Adapted)

Of the many different kinds of dogs now established as British, not a few have had their origin in other lands, whence specimens have been imported into this country, in course of time to be so improved by selection that they have come to be commonly accepted as native breeds. Some are protected from the claim that they are indigenous by the fact that their origin is indicated in their names. No one would pretend that the St. Bernard or the Newfoundland, the Spaniel or the Dalmatian, are of native breed. They are alien immigrants whom we have naturalized, as we are naturalizing the majestic Great Dane, the decorative Borzoi, the alert Schipperke, and the frowning Chow-Chow, which are of such recent introduction that they must still be regarded as half-acclimatised foreigners. But of the antiquity of the Mastiff there can be no doubt. He is the oldest of our British dogs, cultivated in these islands for so many centuries that the only difficulty concerning his history is that of tracing his descent, and discovering the period when he was not familiarly known.

It is possible that the Mastiff owes his origin to some remote ancestor of alien strain. The Assyrian kings possessed a large dog of decided Mastiff type, and used it in the hunting of lions; and credible authorities have perceived a similarity in size and form between the British Mastiff and the fierce Molossian dog of the ancient Greeks. It is supposed by many students that the breed was introduced into early Britain by the adventurous Phoenician traders who, in the sixth century B.C., voyaged to the Scilly Islands and Cornwall to barter their own commodities in exchange for the useful metals. Knowing the requirements of their barbarian customers, these early merchants from Tyre and Sidon are believed to have brought some of the larger *pugnaces*, which would be readily accepted by the Britons to supplant, or improve, their courageous but undersized fighting dogs.

Before the invasion by Julius Caesar, 55 B.C., the name of Britain was little known to the Romans, and it is not to be wondered at that Virgil makes no reference to British dogs; but Gratius Faliscus, writing in the eighth year of the Christian era, recorded that the *pugnaces* of Epirus—the true Molossian dogs—were pitted against the *pugnaces* of Britain, which overpowered them. Gratius further indicates that there were two kinds of the British *pugnaces*, a large and a smaller, suggesting the existence of both the Bulldog and the Mastiff, the latter being employed to protect flocks and herds. Strabo, writing some thirty years later, refers to British dogs used in hunting and in warfare, and, mentioning the *pugnaces*, he especially remarks that they had flabby lips and drooping ears.

The courage of the "broad mouthed dogs of Britain" was recognised and highly prized by the Romans, who employed them for combat in the amphitheatre. Many writers have alleged that in order to secure the best specimens, the Roman Emperors appointed a special officer, Procurator Cynegii, who was stationed at Winchester and entrusted with the duty of selecting and exporting Mastiffs from England to Rome. This statement is frequently repeated by persons who have mistaken the word *cynoecii* for *cynegii*, and confounded the title of a weaver's agent with that of an exporter of dogs. An officer appointed to ship fighting Mastiffs to Rome would have been procurator Pugnacium vel Molossorum.

In Anglo-Saxon times every two villeins were required to maintain one of these dogs for the purpose of reducing the number of wolves and other wild animals. This would indicate that the Mastiff was recognized as a capable hunting dog; but at a later period his hunting instincts were not highly esteemed, and he was not regarded as a peril to preserved game; for in the reign of Henry III, the Forest Laws, which prohibited the keeping of all other breeds by unprivileged persons, permitted the Mastiff to come within the precincts of a forest, imposing, however, the condition that every such dog should have the claws of the fore feet removed close to the skin. A scrutiny was held every third year to ascertain that this law was strictly obeyed.

The name Mastiff was probably applied to any massively built dog. It is not easy to trace the true breed amid the various names which it owned. Molossus, Alan, Alaunt, Tie-dog, Bandog (or Band-dog), were among the number. In the "Knight's Tale," Chaucer refers to it as the Alaunt:

"Aboute his chaar ther wenten white alauntz,
Twenty and mo, as grete as any steer,
To hunten at the leoun or the deer,
And folwed hym, with mosel faste y-bounde,
Colered of gold, and touettes fyléd rounde."

The names Tie-dog and Bandog intimate that the Mastiff was commonly kept for guard, but many were specially trained for baiting bears, imported lions, and bulls. The sport of bear-baiting reached its glory in the sixteenth century. Queen Elizabeth was fond of witnessing these displays of animal conflict, and during her progresses through her realm a bear-baiting was a customary entertainment at the places such as Kenilworth and Hatfield at which she rested. Three trained Mastiffs were accounted a fair match against a bear, four against a lion; but Lord Buckhurst, Elizabeth's ambassador to France in 1572, owned a great Mastiff which, unassisted, successfully baited a bear, a leopard, and a lion, and pulled them all down.

In the representations of the Mastiff in the paintings of the sixteenth and seventeenth centuries, the dog was usually shown with a white blaze up the face and an undershot jaw, the ears were cropped and the tail was shortened. Barnaby Googe in 1631 gave a description of the Bandog for the house which enables us to apprehend what it was like in the time of Charles I—a monarch who admired and kept the breed.

"First, the Mastie that keepeth the house. For this purpose you must provide you such a one as hath a large and mightie body, a great and shrill voyce, that both with his barking he may discover, and with his sight dismaye the theefe, yea, being not seene, with the horror of his voice put him to flight. His stature must be neither long nor short, but well set; his head, great; his eyes, sharp and fiery, either browne or grey; his lippes, blackish, neither turning up nor hanging too much down; his mouth black and wide; his neather jaw, fat, and coming out of it on either side a fang appearing more outward than his other teeth; his upper teeth even with his neather, not hanging too much over, sharpe, and hidden with his lippes; his countenance, like a lion; his breast, great and shag hayrd; his shoulders, broad; his legges, bigge; his tayle, short; his feet, very great. His disposition must neither be too gentle nor too curst, that he neither faune upon a theefe nor flee upon his friends; very waking; no gadder abroad, nor lavish of his mouth, barking without cause; neither maketh it any matter though he be not swifte, for he is but to fight at home, and to give warning of the enemie."

Coming to more recent times, there is constant record of the Mastiff having been kept and carefully bred for many generations in certain old families. One of the oldest strains of Mastiffs was that of Lyme Hall, in Cheshire. They were large, powerful dogs, and longer in muzzle than those which we are now accustomed to see. Mr. Kingdon, who was an ardent Mastiff breeder fifty years ago, maintained that this strain had been preserved without any outcross whatever. On the other hand, it has been argued that this is a statement impossible to prove, as no record of pedigrees was kept. One well-known breeder of former years goes further than this, and states that Mr. Legh had admitted to him that an outcross had been resorted to.

Another old and valuable strain was that of the Mastiffs kept by the Duke of Devonshire at Chatsworth. It is to these two strains that the dogs of the present day trace back.

Crown Prince [bred in Mr. Woolmore's kennels] was a fawn dog with a Dudley nose and light eye, and was pale in muzzle, and whilst full credit must be given to him for having sired many good Mastiffs, he must be held responsible for the faults in many specimens of more recent years. Unfortunately, he was indiscriminately bred from with the result that in a very short time breeders found it impossible to find a Mastiff unrelated to him. The registered pedigree of Crown Prince is by Young Prince by Prince, but the correctness of this pedigree was disputed at the time.

Painting of Chatsworth's Lion. Attributed to T. Hard, 1801.

26

Mr. Beaufoy's Beau proved his claim to be considered a pillar of the stud book by siring Beaufort, unquestionably one of the best Mastiffs of the past twenty years. He was a frequent winner both in this country and in America, where he was placed at stud for a time.

Cardinal was a rich, dark brindle, and one of the most successful sires of his day. He inherited his colour from his dam, a daughter of Wolsey. If for no other reason, Cardinal deserves special mention, as it is mainly due to him that the brindle colour in Mastiffs has been preserved, for I believe that I shall not be wrong in saying that every prize winning brindle of recent years is a direct descendant of this dog.

It is to be deplored that ever since the era of Crown Prince there has been a perceptible diminution in the number of good examples of this fine old English breed, and that from being an admired and fashionable dog, the Mastiff has so declined in popularity that few are to be seen either at exhibitions or in breeders' kennels. At the Crystal Palace in 1871 there were as many as sixty-three Mastiffs on show, forming a line of benches two hundred yards long, and not a bad one among them; whereas at a dog show held twenty-five years later, where more than twelve hundred dogs were entered, not a single Mastiff was benched.

Ch. Ballyherugh's Cormac O'Con ("Thunder"), owned by Gary Wallace, and puppy.

The difficulty of obtaining dogs of unblemished pedigree and superlative type may partly account for this decline, and another reason of unpopularity may be that the Mastiff requires so much attention to keep him in condition that without it he is apt to become indolent and heavy. Nevertheless, the mischief of breeding too continuously from one strain, such as that of Crown Prince, has to some extent been eradicated, and we have had many splendid Mastiffs since his time.

Mr. Robert Leadbetter has also been prominent among the owners of this magnificent breed. His kennel at Haslemere Park is one of the largest at present in England. He started by purchasing Elgiva, a well-known and unbeaten champion who won many specials open to other breeds as well as her own. It is to be regretted that Elgiva failed to contribute progeny towards the continuance of her kind. Among other Mastiffs owned by Mr. Leadbetter may be mentioned Marcella, a bitch descended from Captain Piddocke's strain, and Prince Sonderberg, one of Mr. Laguhee's breeding by Mellnotte out of Nell. Prince Sonderberg's recent death has unfortunately deprived us of a dog which might have won distinction.

Opinions seem to differ as to whether the Mastiff should have a level mouth or be somewhat undershot. Personally I prefer a level mouth, and should always try to get it if possible, and I am inclined to think that many who uphold the undershot jaw are in agreement with me, and would prefer the level mouth were the difficulty of combining it with squareness of muzzle not so great. There can be little doubt that more Mastiffs are bred with undershot jaws than without, and there is no gainsaying the fact that many, if not most, of the best specimens of the breed have possessed undershot jaws.

Size is a quality very desirable in this breed. The height of many dogs of olden days was from thirty-two to thirty-three inches. The height should be obtained rather from great depth of body than length of leg. A leggy Mastiff is very undesirable. Thirty inches may be taken as a fair average height for dogs, and bitches somewhat less. Many of Mr. Lukey's Mastiffs stood 32 inches and over; Mr. Green's Monarch was over 33 inches, The Shah 32 inches, and Cardinal 32 inches.

The method of rearing a Mastiff has much to do with its ultimate size, but it is perhaps needless to say that the selection of the breeding stock has still more to do with this. It is therefore essential to select a dog and bitch of a large strain to obtain

Extremes Meet. A photograph by T. Fall which was reproduced in the August 19, 1922, issue of *Country Life*.

Ch. Vyking Athelwulf of Al Salyng (England, 1956).

large Mastiffs. It is not so necessary that the dogs themselves should be so large as that they come from a large strain. The weight of a full-grown dog should be anything over 160 lb. Many Mastiffs have turned the scale at 180 lb. The Shah, for instance, was 182 lb. in weight, Scawfell over 200 lb.

I am not an advocate for forcing young stock, and I have frequently noticed that in the case of puppies of extraordinary weight, we have seldom heard of any of them attaining any unusual size when full grown. The fact is that these puppies make their growth early in life and stop growing just at the time other puppies are beginning to fill out and develop. There are, of course, exceptions to this. For instance, Orlando weighed 140 lb. when only eight months old. A Mastiff puppy of ten months should have the appearance of a puppy, and not of a full-grown dog. A dog should go on growing until he is three years of age, and many continue to improve after that.

Colour is, to a great extent, a matter of taste. The two colours recognized at the present time are brindle and fawn. The former is considered by those who have given the question most attention to have been the original colour of the breed. Black Mastiffs are spoken of as having been known in years gone by, and occasionally we hear of a dog of this colour having been seen even now. I have never come across one myself, although I have often seen brindle puppies so dark they might have been mistaken for black; nor can I call to mind having heard in recent years of a dog of this colour whose pedigree was known. A correspondent in the *Live Stock Journal* spoke of having seen a black dog of Mastiff type, which was not of pure blood, and went on to say that "when I was paying a visit to the Willhayne kennels, in the summer of 1879, I remember Mr. Kingdon showing me a coal-black bitch of the Lyme Hall breed. She had not a white hair on her, and I was surprised at her colour. She was not at all large."

It is stated that Charles I advertised for a lost "Bob-tailed Black Mastiff," and from the correspondence that took place some years ago upon the subject of the colour of Mastiffs, it is evident that black was by no means an unknown colour at one time. Red was another colour that was in evidence thirty or forty years ago, but it has been allowed to die out, and I have not seen a Mastiff of that colour, whose pedigree could be depended upon, for many years. By crossing blacks and reds, it would no doubt have been possible to produce brindles; this is the case in cattle, and there seems no reason why it should not be so in Mastiffs—in fact, it is asserted that this system of breeding was resorted to many years ago.

Although, as I have said, brindle was the original colour, and was an ordinary one in Mastiffs in the early part of the last century, its place was gradually usurped by the fawn, and twenty-five years or so ago there was great risk of the colour becoming extinct. Mr. J. Hutchings kept a kennel of Mastiffs of this colour, but the type of his dogs did not meet the views of the breeders of the day. Wolsey (5,315), by Rajah out of Mr. Hanbury's Queen (2,396), a magnificent brindled bitch, was about the only dog of note in those days, but his stud services could not be obtained by breeders generally, and so it devolved upon Wolsey's grandson Cardinal to perpetuate the colour. Within the last five years there have been more brindles exhibited than fawns, judging by the fact that more of the former have won prizes than the latter.

White is not a desirable colour, but it will frequently appear on the chest and feet, and in some cases puppies are born with white running some distance up the leg. This, however, disappears almost entirely—or, at any rate, to a great extent—as the puppy grows up.

Light eyes, which detract so much from the appearance of a Mastiff, were very prevalent a few years ago, and, judging from some of the young stock exhibited recently, there seems a great risk of them becoming so again. When this eye appears in a brindle it is even more apparent than in a fawn; the remedy is to breed these dogs to brindles with a good dark eye, and of a strain possessing this quality.

Goliath of Kisimu, winning First at Ox Ridge Kennel Club Show, September 23, 1967. Bred by Mrs. Irene Creigh (England). Owned by Mr. Peter Gaar.

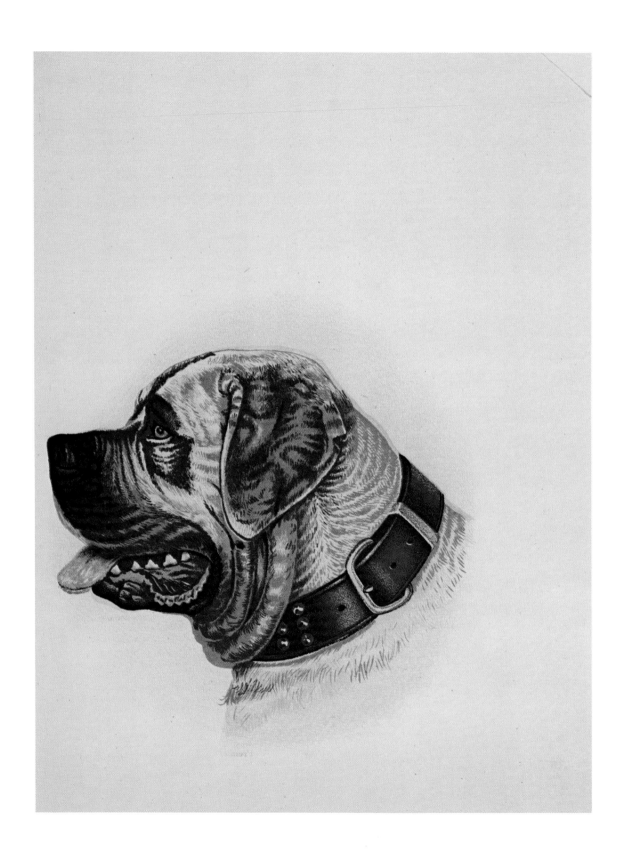

Dr. L. S. Forbes Winslow's Mastiff Crown Prince.

Chapter Five

More History of the Breed

Much of what has been written about the origins of the Mastiff breed is contradictory and controversial. *The History of the Mastiff* by M. B. Wynn, published in 1886, is the first and only important book written about the breed and is looked upon by many as being completely correct in all statements. Mr. James Watson, in his *The Dog Book*, published in 1906, refutes a great many of Mr. Wynn's findings. It is interesting to give you both sides of the picture and let you make up your own mind as to which author you feel is correct. Obviously I cannot give you Mr. Wynn's book in its entirety, but I will endeavor to select and adapt the passages most pertinent to the subject.

"The theory or opinion I hold, is that the English mastiff from the earliest times has existed in Britain, in its purity resembling in many respects a vast bulldog, being the ancestor of that breed. Such being the true pugnaces peculiar to Britian and Gaul mentioned by the historians, and by crossing these with larger breeds, particularly the Asiatic mastiff (introduced probably by the Phoenicians) and other large races of pugnaces, as the white alan or war dogs of the Alani, a large variety of the mastiff was formed, which often became crossed with the boarhounds and other large breeds, as example the Kerry beagle and old Southern hound; to its detriment. Whereas whenever crossed back with its dwarfed descendant the bulldog, manifest improvement in all points except mere height has been obtained.

"The English mastiff and English bulldog present affinity of character possessed in common only by the Spanish bulldog, of any known race of dog, character which is absent even in the Asiatic mastiff. This stamps these varieties as peculiarly European, and places the English bulldog as the most typical of the European mastiff group, and simply unique in its characteristics.

"Before proceeding further it may perhaps render the subject more easy of comprehension, if the history of the Asiatic mastiff is briefly traced from the earliest times up to the present.

"It would be difficult to denominate any precise home of the Asiatic mastiff, or give any more generic name to embrace the allophylian varieties than that from their distinctive features, they must at once be classed as belonging more or less to the mastiff family.

"Their geographical position however has extended from the Caucasian ranges through the valleys of the Elburz mountains, and onwards through the north of Turkistan to the Himalayas, and thence northwards over the vast area of Tibet, the Shan districts, Mongolia and Siberia.

"That a true Asiatic mastiff has existed from very remote ages, is proved by their figures represented on Assyrian sculptures some 650 years B.C. These show the broad short truncated muzzle of the true mastiff, the lips being deeply pendulous, and the loose skin down the sides of the face falling in heavy folds. The ears being wholly pendent, and the dewlap very pronounced (which seems very characteristic to the Asiatic mastiff in its purity), the body cylindrical and heavy, and the limbs extremely massive, the stern mostly carried upwards over the back in a hoop-like curve.

"The next historical mention of the breed is when in 326 B.C. Alexander the Great crossed the Indus—and that mighty conqueror appears to have been the introducer of them into Greece, as before his time the true mastiff with pendent ears appears to have been unknown.

"Of later years these Asiatic mastiffs appear to have degenerated greatly in many districts, owing seemingly to having been crossed with the sharper muzzled smaller breeds owned by the inhabitants of Central Asia, and the finest specimens that have come before European notice have been of Tibetan extraction, so much so, that the Asiatic mastiff has generally become denominated the Tibet mastiff.

"Some years ago I met with a gentleman who had seen many of these dogs brought down to Calcutta for sale by the Bhotans, and he said that they resembled the Newfoundland far more than the English mastiffs, and that the heads of all the specimens that he saw were pointed and wolfish. In color they were generally of a dusky black, with light tan paws, and that they stood not above 27 or 28 inches at shoulder, and in his opinion, had little claim to be considered mastiffs.

"Dogs of a more distinct mastiff type are found in Mongolia, some of a silver-grey colour with long hair and fine brush-like stern.

"The term for the mastiff among some naturalists, is the molossus, originating with our early writers, who chose to think that the classic writers meant a mastiff, in the sense we now use the word, whereas the molossus was not in reality a mastiff. Many people therefore erroneously think the word

Titan Midas winning at a show on March 31, 1968, when he was nine months and one day old. Judge, Mr. Vincent Perry.

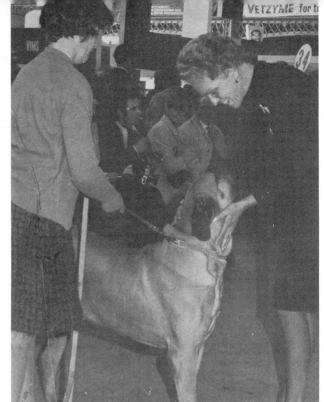

At the Crufts Show, Olympia, London, 1970. Judge, Mrs. Marie A. Moore.

At left, Prince Valiant D'Orleans, owned by Mrs. Frank Greco.

Mooreleigh Za Za, Best of Breed at 1972 National Capital Kennel Club Show. Owner, Mrs. Pat Weidenkeller.

molossus necessarily means a mastiff, whereas the Greeks only became acquainted with the true mastiff about the time of the Macedonian conquest at 336 B.C., being about 300 years after the breed was cultivated by the Assyrian kings.

"History informs us that the Molossus was the name of a king of a people living in Epirus, who took the name of Molossi from him, and the district obtained the name of Molossis, where were the mountains of Selli or Suli. This country became famous for its dogs as guardians of flock and homestead, and they were imported to Rome, and became well known under the name of canes molossi.

"Dogs of a true mastiff type have existed from the earliest times, and it has been conjectured that the Phoenicians introduced the Assyrian or Asiatic mastiff into Britain. The Phoenician traders would have to bring articles for exchange calculated to suit the taste of their British producers of tin, and what more likely than seeing the courageous but somewhat undersized pugnaces or fighting dogs, owned by the Britons, that they should bring as an article of barter some of the larger pugnaces or mastiffs of Asia, of which modern scholarship and research renders it presumable they would be fully cognizant of.

"In this larger variety, used to guard the doors of the houses of the Britons, and to protect their flocks and herds, we can plainly trace the mastiff and its superiority over the true molossus.

"Arrian, who wrote about A.D. 130, and whose work was translated by the Rev. W. Dansey in 1831, mentions the pugnaces of Britain and Gaul in his Cynegeticus, observing that they were getting scarce in their purity, having been much crossed with the larger and swifter breeds. This mention on Arrian's part of the crossing of the pure British pugnaces, to obtain greater size, shows very clearly how the British mastiff was manufactured, and accounts for the breed being mentioned by various subsequent writers as the greater and lesser sort.

"However, there have been some writers and dog fanciers in England [who have endeavored] to make out that the English mastiff exists in its purity and is quite a distinct family from the courageous English bulldog. The two breeds nevertheless have evidently arisen from a common origin.

"From the father of English classics, Dan Chaucer, we read that there existed in Britain in his day a variety of dog called the Alan, which appears also to have been termed Alauntes. What these were exactly is not very clear. Modern writers have mauled and twisted this word Alan, and the breed it designated, without proving or suggesting anything satisfactory, or even probable, still, the term must have had a derivation, and I am inclined to think it is probably the ancient British name for the mastiff (although of Slavonic origin and perhaps Phoenician introduction). The Spanish still have the word in use under the Spanish form Alano, and curiously enough showing the close relationship between the two breeds, apply it to denote either a mastiff or bulldog.

"I think it is probable that the word Alan was the Phoenician term to denote the Asiatic mastiff and was introduced by them into Britain as well as Spain.

"After the evidences of the British mastiff left us by the poets and artists at the time when the Roman supremacy over Britain was in the height of its culture and civilization, scanty are any traces of the breed until after the Norman conquest.

"The Saxons, a race of rude warriors, terse in their phraseology and possessed of little skill in sculpture or carving, apparently found the British mastiff used principally as a watch dog. Of the mastiff during the Saxon times, there is next to no record, beyond their terse barbarian name for the breed, that of 'bandog,' evidently bestowed on account of the use they found the mastiff put to in this country.

"The mastiff has commonly borne the name of bandog from the time of Canute to the last century; Ban-dog or band-dog is of true Saxon origin, from banda, a chain, or any narrow ligament by which a thing is bound, and doc, a dog, hence banda-doc, or band-dog, a chained dog, and it was the recognized term for the mastiff.

"The word mastiff is evidently of Norman introduction, and is probably a Gallic form of the Latin word massivus, the 't' being interchanged for the 's'; the word being derived from massa, a mass, and applied to the breed on account of the thickset, massive, or masty form of the animal. It is specially worthy of note that both the Armoric and Spanish have the word in the form mastin, and in ancient French it was the same, having become contracted into matin. The Italian has also the same word with the vowel ending suffixed, mastino.

"The term mastiff until after the age of Elizabeth was used for both mastiff and bulldog, and it was not until the time of Ben Johnson that the word bandog fell into disuse, except to define a mongrel watchdog. The bulldog became defined

Reveille Lancelot at twenty-two months of age. Owned by Mr. and Mrs. Jeffrey Short, Chicago, Illinois.

by the sport it was used for, and the word mastiff applied only to the breed we now understand by that name.

"The following extract is from the charter of the forest of Henry 3rd, 'of keeping dogs within the forest and expeditating the same, and the forfeiture for keeping them unexpeditated therein.

" 'And therefore farmers and substantial freeholders dwelling within the forest, may keep mastiffs for the defence of their houses within the same, providing such mastiffs be expeditated according to the laws of the forest.' From this, we may see the early encouragement which was given towards keeping the mastiff as a guard for premises.

"Agincourt, as well as a landmark in English history, furnishes also an important piece of history connected with the English mastiff, for the legend runs that on October 25th, 1415, on Agincourt's bloody field, a favourite mastiff bitch of Sir Peers Leigh (Knight of Lyme Hall) protected her master from molestation as he lay wounded on the field during the night after the battle, until some English soldiers found him, and he was removed to Paris, where he died, and the mastiff, who was in whelp at the time, had a litter of puppies. Sir Peer's body was brought back to Lyme for burial, and the bitch and whelps along with it.

"The puppies were kept by the family out of a sort of gratitude for the fidelity of their dam, and from them, with crosses, introduced from time to time, the breed is said to have been kept up at Lyme Hall until the present time.

"The family appear to have kept up the breed by crossing with specimens in the vicinity, and Lancashire has always been noted for the number of bandogs kept to guard its grounds. But at Lyme Hall no record appears ever to have been kept of the lineage of the race, neither has any purity in type seemingly been cultivated, and the breed has generally presented animals approaching the boarhound in character, being too long in the head, pointed in the muzzle, high on the leg and light in body, for mastiff purity.

"The mastiff, being present with Sir Peers Leigh at Agincourt, shows that at that date the breed was often the favorite companion and guard of the wealthy, and their courage was, to use the words of Shakespeare, simply unmatchable—a characteristic the bulldog has kept up, if not its larger relative the mastiff, in all instances.

"It will be seen that the legitimate uses of the mastiff among the Britons were to defend their homes and property, and also to assist in driving cattle, while in times of war they afforded a guard for the women and chariots. The Romans fought animals in their amphitheatres, and from their savage fondness for such sights as gladiatorial shows and pitting animals against each other in all probability arose the introduction of baiting animals with dogs in Britain. Principally the mastiff was used to bait the bear, but at times even the horse and ass suffered, the latter animal furnishing a spirited combat.

"It will readily be seen for baiting purposes, while size in the mastiff meant power, at the same time mere size without proportionate muscular development and bulk, with the characteristic short head and powerful jaws, was not the standard either aimed at then or to be aimed at now; and some otherwise fair judges have fallen into the error of considering size an essential in the mastiff, and have mistaken the true mastiff type, preferring the more extenuated type, derived from a boarhound or Great Danish cross.

"The 16th century opens like the dawn of day, throwing a brightening light on the history of most things in England of that period, and among them, that of the mastiff is revealed much clearer. With the introduction of printing and illustrating by woodcuts, we get many more examples of the form of the mastiff of that date.

"Berjeau's work contains a cut of a mastiff bitch and whelps. The original was drawn previous to 1591. The bitch is a short headed, heavy muzzled animal, with over large ears. Her limbs are short and stout. The five puppies vary much in character, one being a short round-headed, short-tailed promising little fellow, such a one as any breeder would like to possess, while the larger brother is indifferent in head, showing at that date even, in the same litter, puppies varied in size and type, and that unless the breeder is careful to select nearest to the ideal, the type will degenerate, unless the surer rule of the survival of the fittest is put into execution, which in the mastiff of that date meant the selection of the best performers in the bear garden, whereat the shortest headed and most muscular were sure to bear the palm.

"James 1st gave little encouragement to painting, but Charles 1st tried to introduce a love for painting and fine art generally, and owing to his patronage, he has bequeathed to us one portrait of a mastiff in his reign; for in about 1638 Vandyck made a painting of the children of Charles 1st, together with a large and somewhat mastiff-like dog. From the children's statue it is easy to discern at once that the dog was of vast size, he seems to have been a deep red fawn with the usual white on the face and legs, his ears were cropped somewhat roughly, and not so close as in most instances. I have some doubts of its being really an English mastiff, thinking it very probable to have been an importation, having too much of the boarhound character about it for mastiff purity.

"From the foregoing pictures we see it was the custom to crop the ears and shorten the tail of the mastiff in Charles 1st's day, which fashion remained up to 1835 at least; Squire Waterton's Tiger and Mr. Lukey's first mastiff Countess being thus mutilated, and from the boarhound paintings we see it was also the Continental custom.

"It is worthy of notice that in nearly all the early paintings of the mastiff, they are marked with the white blaze up the face and white legs, also that black was a mastiff color about 1600.

"In 1753 was born Thomas Bewick, a man destined to reanimate the method of illustrating works by woodcuts; he has left many delineations of the English mastiff. In his *History of Quadrupeds* the mastiff is represented with ears uncropped. This, like nearly every specimen of the mastiff depicted by Bewick, has white on the face, neck, ribs, flank, legs, and stern. This amount of white in all mastiffs of that and preceding date may have been due to the white stirp of Alan blood, but more probably to a great extent to the amount of inbreeding then practised."

The balance of Mr. Wynn's book is concerned with tracing the pedigrees of the various Mastiffs known at that time, but since few records were kept, even in the larger kennels, it is purely conjecture for the most part.

In his *The Dog Book*, published in 1906, Mr. James Watson states in part:

"Mr. Wynn's 'History of the Mastiff' is the best work on the breed, but it should be read with caution by persons who have not made a thorough investigation and read for themselves. The reason is that while he has brought together a most valuable collection of data and gives many valuable references to olden-time books, manuscripts and illustrations, he was so rabidly impressed by the conviction that the mastiff was a very old breed and yet thoroughly English that he twisted every available fact or stringing together of two or three words to bear out his line of argument. Unfortunately for Mr. Wynn and those who have published similar suppositions, the foundation upon which they built was a quicksand. Their whole structure is based upon the mastiff of the earliest writings being the mastiff of our day, and there they are wrong.

"Before showing what the mastiff was five hundred years ago, it will be well to consider what the meaning or derivation of the word mastiff is. Our etymologists are in a much better position to give the correct interpretation of old words than their predecessors and the up-to-date meaning of mastiff is a mongrel or cross-bred dog.

"The mastins were used in wild boar hunting, as we find in Gaston de Phoebus, but not because they were so much more courageous than other dogs, such as the alaunt, which was the high-class dog; but in order to avoid the risk of losing the more valuable dogs, these keen-fighting, half-bred dogs were also used to run in at the boar at bay and at the wolf.

"The evidence we shall present regarding the dog called the mastiff before and up to 1800 does not conclusively show any great dissimilarity between the mastiff and the bulldog of that time. We mean by that the dividing line was not specially marked by a great dissimilarity of size or of type. The bulldogs differed in size and the mastiffs also, making them closely allied when it came to the larger bulldog and the smaller mastiff.

"When the name of mastiff or any of its equivalents was used in England in the early days there is nothing to show that the dogs held very high rank. Some dogs that did so were called mastiffs, that we admit, but these were individual dogs and not indicative of the breed, which filled many use-

Mooreleigh Gregory. Owned by Mrs. Eve Olsen.

ful positions, but nearly all inferior to those of the dogs of the chase, kept by English nobility.

"At the period covered by Caius, 1550, the mastiff was undoubtedly the largest of the English dogs. He says of the mastiff that he is usually tied and is mighty, gross and fat-fed. It is not necessary to imagine that they were anything like the size of our mastiffs. Indeed, from illustrations which appeared during the next hundred years, in representations of attacks on bears, they were apparently not much larger than a setter. Of course much heavier and stronger but no taller. Active, powerful dogs with square-shaped heads.

"It is probable that in the case of the larger mastiffs which were kept as watch-dogs, and were bred here and there by noblemen, that there was a far more definite attempt to gain size and establish type, and to this we owe the development of the dog into the mastiff of 1800. There is no reason to doubt that at the close of the eighteenth century there was in England a large square-headed dog, frequently marked with white and varying in body colour from fawn to black, with brindles of various shades. But the name mastiff ranged down to dogs of large bulldog size. [Comparing Bewick's bulldog and mastiff,] it will be seen that there is extremely little difference between them.

"That this mastiff of Bewick's was typical of all the mastiffs of his day is quite out of the question; but that it was accepted as an excellent illustration of quite a number of mastiffs is undoubtedly correct, for it was copied for many years.

"To support Bewick we have a good mastiff in a Reinagle painting dating from 1803. This dog shows a great deal more quality and breeding than the rather common though well proportioned dog of Bewick.

"Thus far there has been considerable groping along a very indistinct path, but we can now make use of a broad thoroughfare of knowledge. Mr. Wynn was a man of indefatigable research, and when it comes to facts he could obtain first-hand, he let nothing interfere in getting them from the parent source. The extraordinary thing, which he clearly proves, although he does not know it, is that we owe our mastiff to a few obscurely picked up dogs of unknown origin and from others that were either half-bred Great Danes or dogs known as Alpine mastiffs, that being the name for the St. Bernard about 1820.

"The Lyme Hall strain was undoubtedly of alaunt descent. Such of the Lyme Hall strain as we have seen lacked very much the short face of the mastiff, and were light in body, being altogether too much of the Dane in type.

"It will be seen what very slight support there is for the claim that the mastiff is descended in all its purity from a magnificent lot of dogs of the highest breeding for many generations and through several centuries. The patent facts are that from a number of dogs of various types of English watch-dogs and baiting dogs, running from 26 inches to 29 or perhaps 30 inches in height, crossed with continental dogs of Great Dane and of old fashioned St. Bernard type, the mastiff has been elevated through the efforts of English breeders to the dog he became about twenty years ago.

"We have shown very clearly, we think, that the mastiff of 1885 was a very different animal in accentuation of head type from the early show dogs. We cannot give the space that really should be devoted to even a mention by names and will content ourselves with a reference to Crown Prince whose career was phenomenal. Crown Prince's eyes were a very decided yellow and were anything but pleasing in expression. He also had a flesh coloured nose [and was very straight in the stifle]. Yet such was the craze for the short, square head, at that time, that he had an almost unbeaten record, and . . . of course, he was bred from very largely.

"The mastiff should be a free and easy mover, but fast work is not an essential, hence speed lines are not called for; but to support the weight of the dog we must have good legs and the soundest feet: weakness there means a useless dog."

So ends the observations of Mr. Watson. Actually all this old history has very little bearing on the Mastiff of today because the breed was very nearly exterminated by World War II.

The following is adapted from the minutes of the Old English Mastiff Club:

"On 25th October, 1946, an Open meeting was held in London which was the first time members had met since 1939. Fifteen people attended and pledged themselves to do all in their power to save the breed from extinction. The first thing was to trace all the mastiffs in the country and, if possible, arrange for mating and breeding operations. For several reasons these plans largely failed, mainly because most of the 20 Mastiffs that were discovered were too old for breeding and a terrible wave of Distemper was raging at that time. A dog called Taurus [Note: "Templecomb Taurus" was never established as a Mastiff], whose master had been killed in a bombing raid, had been rescued and he sired three litters before dying at an early age. Of these 18 puppies only one survived. Other misfortunes occurred and at the end of 1947 only 7 Mastiffs survived. Mrs. Dickin, the Secretary, visited America in this year but found the breed very nearly extinct there and [of such poor quality] she returned without making any purchases. In 1948, Mr. and Mrs. Mellish of Victoria, British Columbia, sent the Club two puppies. In 1949 we were able to report that a total of 15 Mastiffs were in the country. By the end of 1950 there were about 50 Mastiffs and it may well be claimed that the breed has again been established in this country."

It is only logical to assume that the Mastiff was crossed with Danes, Bullmastiffs and St. Bernards as recently as twenty-five or twenty-six years ago. This is proved by the "throw-backs" that appear in Mastiff litters even now, and the only solution or hope of establishing a pure strain is for the present-day breeders to cull their litters rigorously, which, of course, they won't do.

The first conclusive evidence of the Mastiff in America comes in the early 1880's when the breed began to appear at the bench shows. Still, it was not until 1885 that the first specimens were registered in the American Kennel Club stud book. There were only nine specimens registered at that time. This modest beginning gave no indication of the rapid climb to popularity that was to follow. In 1889, the Mastiff reached the greatest proportionate popularity it ever has attained in the United States. There were 373 specimens registered. Following the peak year of 1889, the breed began to decline slowly. By the time of World War I, it had almost disappeared from sight. It

Titan Tangela at seven-and-a-half months of age (May 23, 1959). Judge, Mr. Frank Foster Davis.

remained in comparative obscurity until 1935. In that year, there were twenty-five registrations, but there was little breeding stock available. However, slowly but surely, the breed is becoming more popular again, for there were 810 registrations recorded by The American Kennel Club in 1976.

An understanding of pedigrees and the existing bloodlines, the willingness to cooperate with one another, and the determination to eliminate the mentally and physically unsound individuals from any breeding program are the first steps to be taken towards establishing a worth-while strain of Mastiff which should stand high on the list of Working breeds.

Beowulf and Sheba, owned by Mrs. Eve Olsen.

Assyrians Leading Mastiffs to a Hunt.

Assyrians with Mastiffs.

The "Dog of Alcibiades."

Mastiffs Hunting Wild Horses.

Chapter Six

The Mastiff in Ancient Times, by Edmund G. Oliver

(From *The Kennel Gazette*— October 1931)

Much has been written upon the early history of Mastiffs, but I venture to hope that the following remarks may assist in throwing some fresh light upon a somewhat obscure subject.

The Mastiff, in something like his present mould, appears to have existed from the earliest dawn of history. Evidence of this is afforded by the admirable bas reliefs to be seen in the Assyrian Rooms at the British Museum, displaying the dogs of Kings Esarhaddon and Ashur-bani-pal used for hunting wild horses, and lions, in the seventh century B.C. I am much indebted to the Department of Egyptian and Assyrian Antiquities, British Museum, for permission to reproduce with this article three striking photographs of portions of these bas-reliefs on which appear several excellent specimens of Assyrian Mastiffs.

These dogs are of a type practically identical with the Mastiff of the present day, though apparently of greater size.

They were evidently highly thought of, and we find that in Assyria the dog was the emblem of the god Gula.

Of great interest, too, are many of the terra-cotta plaques to be found in the wall and table-cases in the same rooms. One of these plaques is stamped with a scene representing a man leading a dog— plainly of mastiff type.

Five more terra-cotta models of Mastiffs of similar type have each the name of the dog inscribed on its left side. Evidently it was not then, as now, customary to give dogs human names, but to name each dog in a way descriptive of his character, or powers. The translations of the names inscribed on these five models are: 1, "Hesitate not; work thy jaws"; 2, "Conqueror of the foe"; 3, "Biter of his opponent"; 4, "Expeller of the wicked"; 5, "The strong of his bark," i.e. "The Loud-bayer."

Another good example of a dog of precisely similar type described as an Indian dog is given by Professor George Rawlinson in his translation of Herodotus (1862) in an illustration.

Similar terra-cotta models of dogs have been frequently dug up, in excavation of the sites of ancient cities in Babylonia. These were formerly considered to be simply models of the hunting dogs of Ashur-bani-pal. But it is now known that the Assyrians were in the habit of burying figures of dogs of different colours under the thresholds of their houses, so that the spirits of the dogs might repel the attacks of evil spirits who might attempt to enter the house.

The number of figures of dogs usually buried under a house was ten, arranged five on each side of the doorway. Each figure of the five on each side of the doorway was of a different colour, viz: white, grey, spotted, red and black. Traces of the colours remain on the models in the Assyrian Room. This curious custom seems to indicate that Mastiffs were valued as watch-dogs from the earliest times.

These Mastiffs are also sometimes represented on cylinders.

Darwin mentions an enormous Mastiff figured on the tomb of the son of Esarhaddon, an Assyrian monument of about 640 B.C.

It seems that dogs of similar type were kept by the ancient Egyptians and Mr. E. C. Ash in his great work on dogs, shows us an illustration which he tells us, dates back to about 2,000 B.C. Aristotle says that the Egyptian dogs were smaller than the Greek.

The history of the Mastiff during Classical times has no doubt been veiled in obscurity, but it is not to be presumed that the breed came suddenly to an end after the fall of the Assyrian Empire, only to appear again in England some centuries later.

There is indeed a considerable amount of evidence that dogs of Mastiff type existed in many parts of the world during the Greek and Roman eras. I propose to sum up all the evidence I have collected on this subject in another place, and to state here shortly a few of the premises.

The following quotations from Philemon Holland's translation of *Pliny's Natural History*, 1601, shows how Mastiffs were used as War Dogs for actual fighting.

"There was a king of the Germanes who was brought back from exile, and recovered his royal state againe by the meanes of 200 dogges that fought for him against all those that made resistance and brought him home maugre his enemies. The Colophonians and Castabaleans" (both peoples inhabiting Asia Minor) "maintained certain squadrons of mastive dogges for their war-service; and those were put in the vaward to make the head and front of the battaile, and were never known to draw backe, and refuse fight. These were the trustiest auxiliaries and aid-souldiers, and never so needie as to call for pay. In a battell when the Cimbrians were defeated, and put all to the sword, their dogges defended the baggage. Yea, and their houses (such as they were) carried ordinarily upon charriots."

Later in the same chapter occurs a description of dogs presented by the King of Albania to Alexander the Great:

"In the voyage that Alexander the Great made into India, the King of Albanie gave him a dogge of an huge and extraordinary bignesse. And Alexander taking great delight and contentment to see so goodly and so faire a dogge; let loose unto him first Beares, afterwaeds wild Bores; and last of all fallow Deere. But this dogge making no reckoning of all this game, lay still couchant, and never stirred nor made at them. This great Commander Alexander, a man of mightie spirit, and high-minded, offended at the lazynesse and cowardice of so great a bodie, commanded that he should be killed, and so he was. News hereof went presently to the King of Albanie. Whereupon he sent unto him a second dogge, with this message—That he should not make trial of this too against such little beasts, but either set a Lion or an Elephant at him; saying moreover that hee had in all but those two of that kind; and if hee were killed likewise, hee were like to have no more of that race and breed. Alexander made no stay, but presently put out a Lion, and immediately he saw his backe broken and all to rent and torne by the dogge. Afterwards he commended to bring forth an Elephant, and in no fight took he greater pleasure than in this; for the dogge at the first with his rough, shagged haire, that overspread his whole bodie, came with full mouth, thundering (as it were) and barking terribly against the Elephant. Soon after he leapeth and flieth upon him, rising and mounting guard against the great beast, now of one side, then of another; maintaining combate right artificially, one while assailing another while avoiding his enemie; and so nimbly he bestirreth from side to side, that with continuall turning about too and fro, the Elephant grew giddie in the head, insomuch as he came tumbling downe, and made the ground to shake under him with his fall."

Other descriptions of fights between dogs and Lions are to be found in Megasthenes, Aelian, Diodorus Siculus, Strabo and Plutarch, and in some respects resemble the well-known descriptions of lion-baiting with Mastiffs in England in Tudor times.

In Strabo's account for example, two Mastiffs were at first set on a Lion. When these were getting the worse of it, two others were launched, and established the equilibrium. This much resembles the equation current in England in Tudor times—four Mastiffs = one Lion.

Mr. M. B. Wynn in his *History of the Mastiff* says that the Canis Molossus of Epirus was not a Mastiff, and that the Greeks only became acquainted with the true Mastiff about the time of the Macedonian Conquest. He gives no authority for this statement, and his work bristles with mistakes to such an extent as to make it entirely unreliable, and practically worthless, at any rate for the early history of the breed. The statue of the "Dog of Alcibiades," of which two photographs are reproduced with this article, affords in itself a sufficient refutation of Wynn's statement.

Ancient Epirus formed part of what is now Albania, and that the Molossi of Epirus maintained their reputation as fighting dogs even in the Middle Ages, is proved by the following extract from the *Travels of William de Rubruquis*, a monk in the service of Louis IX, King of France (St. Louis), who, referring to Albania, says "of which country Isidore reputeth that there are in it dogs of such huge stature, and so fierce, that they are able to fight to match bulls, and to master lions which is true as I was assured by several, who told me that towards the North Ocean they make their dogs draw carts like oxen, on account of their strength."

The truth probably is that the term Canis Molossus included two different types, as Professor Keller points out. One of these was of hound type, similar to the Laconian hound, and the other appearing on the Epiro-Molossian coins is the Mastiff, much more thick set than the Greek hunting dog, with a very ample neck, with huge bone, and heavily built. This type, says Keller, was undoubtedly the Epirot Molossus described by Aristotle in his *History of Animals*.

It is perhaps worthy of remark that the term "Canis Molossus" has always been translated as "Mastiff" amongst others by such great authorities as Du Cange, Galfridus Grammaticus, Stephen Skinner, Camden and Minshaeus.

The Canis Molossus, as he was at the time of the great days of Athens, is perhaps best shown today by the magnificent statue of the "Dog of Alcibiades" at Duncombe Park, Helmsley, the seat of Lord Feversham, by whose courtesy I was able to see the statue, which was purposely unveiled for the purpose, and to whom I am infinitely indebted for the photographs which I am able to reproduce here. Horace Walpole estimated this statue as one of the five finest statues of animals in the

Weatherhill Bellringer. Sire, Jason of Copenore. Dam, Ch. Weatherhill Milf Manetta.

Weatherhill Saga at twelve months of age (October 1963). By Jason of Copenore out of Ch. Weatherhill Milf Manetta.

world. It was restored by Cavaceppi, who attributed it to the great Pheidias, and executed an engraving of it.

A statue of a similar Molossian dog, also entitled the "Dog of Alcibiades," may be seen in the Uffizzi Palace at Florence. Dr. Waagen considers the Duncombe Park Dog more animated, and of more careful workmanship, than the Florentine statue. The "Dog of Alcibiades" is also mentioned by J. J. Winckelmann, who quotes some similar specimens, two in the Pio-Clementino collection, and one in the Chigi Palace, at Rome, two more in the Galleries at Florence, all of which he describes as fine pieces of work, though he rates the Duncombe Park Statue highest as an artistic production.

This dog was, evidently, of Mastiff type. The chest, legs and feet, and the formation of the skull, are exactly similar to the Mastiff of the present day; the bone is even bigger. The statue is in good condition, except that half of the muzzle and the left fore-leg, have been restored. The coat is smooth, except for a ruffle round the neck, and a slightly bushy tail. The statue is a most imposing object of remarkable artistic merit, and is of Parian marble.

Mastiff dogs of precisely similar type were sculptured as sepulchral monuments over tombs.

A good specimen of Hymettan marble may still be seen in the burial-ground near the chapel of the Hagia Trias at Athens, where the dog is lying on the plinth covering the tomb. With uplifted head and forelegs fully extended he appears to be watching over the tomb, a courageous and faithful guardian. A good photograph of this dog is given by Collignon in his well-known work on Greek Sculpture. Similar dogs are sculptured in relief outside tombs at Telmessus and Tlos in Lycia, the dog in each case being posted near the door giving entrance to the funeral vault. Alfred Brueckner gives a fine illustration of a similar dog also in the burial ground near the Hagia Trias Chapel at Athens on a tomb, which is he tells us of the fourth century B.C.

The dog of Alcibiades, and other statues seem to afford conclusive evidence of the existence and popularity of dogs of Mastiff type among the Greeks in the fifth century B.C. and later.

Such a one may have been the dog that guarded so faithfully the body of King Lysimachus, when he lay dead on the plain of Corus.

Montaigne tells us that the name of this dog was Hyrcamus, and that when his master's body was burnt, he took a run and leaped into the flames where he was consumed. He says he got this story

Titan Silver Lace (1970). Owner, Mrs. Barbara Simmons.

Ch. Weatherhill Milf Manetta, owned by Dr. Allison.

from Plutarch, but I have been unable to identify the passage.

Dogs of this type were used as fighting war dogs, and it is likely that it was one of them who took part in the battle of Marathon, where we are told that an Athenian warrior brought his dog with him as his companion-in-arms. Both appeared together in a notable painting at Poecile, thought to be by the hand of Polygnotus, or Nicor. In this picture (unfortunately, as have been all the great Greek paintings, long since destroyed) the dog is described as a noble and conspicuous figure, having attained the highest award for facing danger.

Of Xanthippus' dog which had to be left behind when the Athenians evacuated Athens under stress of the invasion of Xerxes before the battle of Salamis, Plutarch in his *Life of Themistocles*, tells the following story—I quote from Sir Thomas North's translation (1579):—

"There was besides a certain pittie that made mens harts to yerne, when they saw the poore doggs, beasts, and cattell ronne up and downe, bleating, mowing and howling out alowde after their masters, in token of sorowe, when they dyd imbarke. Amongest these, there goeth a straunge tale of Xanthippus dogge, who was Pericles father; which for sorowe his master had left behinde him, dyd cast him self after into the sea, and swimming still by the galleys side wherein his master was, he helde on to the Ile of Salamina, where so sone as the poore curre landed, his breath fayled him, and dyed presently. They saye, at this daye the place called the doggs grave, is the very place where he was buried.

The same story is told in Plutarch's life of M. Porcius Cato, the Censor, with the interesting addition "Amonge other olde Xanthippus buried his dogge on the toppe of a cliffe which is called the dogge's pit till this day."

These mastiff dogs seem to have been used also for the purpose of guarding sheep against wolves. I quote the following from Sir Thomas North's translation of Plutarch's *Life of Demosthenes:*—

"At which time" (the invasion of Alexander the Great) "they wryte that Demosthenes told the people of Athens, the fable of the sheepe and woulves, how that the woulves came on a time, and willed the sheepe, if they woulde have peace with them, to deliver them their Mastives that kept them. And so he compared him selfe, and his companions that travelled for the benefit of the contrie, unto the dogges that kepe the flocks of sheepe, and calling Alexander the woulfe."

Ctesias the Cnidian; who was a contemporary of Xenophon; and if Herodotus lived until 425 B.C., or according to some until 408 B.C., he may also be called a contemporary of Herodotus; lived many years at the Court of Artaxerxes Memnon, King of Persia, and brother of Cyrus the younger, as private physician to the King. He gives an account of dogs, described as Indian dogs, kept by the Cynomolgi, a barbarous tribe in the South of Ethiopia, also known as the Cynomones, and confused by Pliny with the Cynocephali. He tells us that these dogs, perhaps descended from the Babylonian dogs, were of great size, as large as the Hyrcanian breed, and that they fought even with the lion. The Cynomolgi reared a large number of these dogs for the following reason:—

"From the time of the summer solstyce on to mid-winter they are incessantly attacked by herds of wild oxen, coming like a swarm of bees, or a flight of angry wasps, only that the oxen are more numerous by far. They are ferocious withal and proudly defiant, and butt most viciously with their horns. The Cynomolgi, unable to withstand them otherwise, let loose their dogs upon them, which are bred for this express purpose, and these dogs easily overpower the oxen, and worry them to death. Then come the masters, and appropriate to their own use such part of the carcases as they deem fit for food, but they set apart for their dogs all the rest and gratitude prompts them to give this share cheerfully. During the season when they are left unmolested by the oxen, they employ the dogs in hunting other animals. They milk the bitches and this is why they are called Cynomolgi (dog milkers). They drink this milk, just as we drink that of the sheep or goat."

Similar accounts are given by Diodorus Siculus, Aelian, and Polydeuktes.

Interesting is Aristotle's statement that Indian dogs are derived from a cross between the tiger and the dog but from the third cross, for they say that the first race is too fierce. They took the bitches and tied them upon the desert. Many of them are devoured, if the wild animal does not happen to desire sexual intercourse.

It is somewhat surprising to see this statement repeated by Pliny.

No such crossing was of course possible, but the owners of the dogs doubtless found that the repute was a good advertisement. One might perhaps reasonably surmise that these dogs were brindles.

Herodotus tells us that when Tritantaechmes son of Artabazus was Satrap of Babylon under the Persian domination, "he kept so great a number of Indian dogs that four large villages of the plain

Black Mask of Broom Court and Broom Court Nell (1935).

were exempted from all other charges on condition of finding them food."

This Tritantaechmes may have been a son of Artabazus, brother to Darius Hystaspes, King of Persia, or more probably he was the Satrap at the time of Herodotus' visit about 450 B.C.

Oppian in the first of his Cynegetica gives a description of a dog of great size with a flat skull, a knitted frown on his brow, and pendulous lips.

It is said that the Emperor Heliogalalus, that irrational voluptuary, who styled himself Cybele the mother of the gods, and who imitated Mark Antony by driving a chariot drawn by four Lions, sometimes varied his team by substituting "Four Mastive Dogs," or "Four naked wenches causing himself to be drawne by them in pomp and state hee being all naked."

There seems to be no doubt that Mastiffs were found in England by the Romans when they first landed here, and that they were afterwards exported for the purpose of fighting in the colosseum and other amphitheatres.

Mastiffs were also exported from Britain by the Gauls for the purpose of fighting with their armies, and Holinshed says "The Gaules did sometime buy up all our mastiffes, to serve in the forewards of their battels."

The envoys sent by Betuitus, king of the Averni (erroneously called by Appian, king of the Allo-broges) to the Romans, who were at war with them under Cnaeus Domitius, were accompanied by dogs. For dogs were used by the Averni as personal bodyguards.

It is a most interesting question, apparently impossible to be answered with certainty, how Mastiffs first came to our island: for it is hardly to be supposed that they were indigenous here.

It has been suggested that they were introduced by the Phoenicians in the course of their trading with Cornwall, and the Scilly Islands, whence they procured tin by barter. Though this seems to be quite a possible theory, it would appear to be at least equally probable that they were introduced from the Continent. There is a record of trading between England on the one hand, and Gaul and Belgium on the other, anterior to the first Roman invasion, and trade in dogs between these countries certainly flourished during the Augustan age and in the third century A.D.

Ch. Rachel of Ram's Gate, whelped June 5, 1971. Bred, owned, and handled by Judy A. and Dr. Dwayne L. Nash, Lodi, California. Pictured at Santa Barbara Kennel Club Show going Best of Opposite Sex at thirteen months of age under Mrs. Francis Crane.

Friedeswide Oliver, Best of Breed at the Old English Mastiff Club Specialty Show at Pangbourne, Berkshire, England, June 1967. Judge, Marie A. Moore.

Pictured below, left to right, are Raven of Blackroc, Willowledge Gairhart, Ballyherugh's Cormac Mac Art, Ballyherugh's Cormac O'Con, Ballyherugh's Blarney Stone, Goliath of Kisimu, Sampson of 40 Acres, Ballyherugh's Monroe, Willowledge Grindle, and Reveille Juggernaut.

Chapter Seven

Stories About Mastiffs

In A. F. J. de Freville's *Histoire des Chiens Celebres* (1796) we find the following anecdote:

In the terrible winter of 1709, the year of the great battles of Poltava and Malplaquet, when the corn, the vines, the olives, and the fruit trees in France were all frozen, the wolves made terrible ravages in the country and attacked even human beings. One of these ferocious and famishing animals, after having broken a window, entered a cottage in the Forest of Orta, near Angouleme. Two children, one six and the other eight years old, were lying on their bed awaiting their mother, who had gone to fetch some wood to make them a fire. Seeing there was no resistance, the wolf leaped on the bed with the intention of devouring his tender prey.

Seized with fright, the two little boys slid quickly under the mattress and kept themselves hidden there without breathing. So near to the prey for which he longed and unable to seize it immediately, the wolf became more animated. He set to work to tear the mattress in pieces with great bites, and soon would have done this, as well as the sheets.

Feeble as these obstacles were against such an attack, they yet served to secure the safety of the two little children. While the furious wolf was attacking their entrenchments, an enormous Mastiff which had followed the mother returned in time to save them. The traces of the fetid odor of the wolf were picked up by the dog more than a hundred paces from the house towards which the woman, laden with her faggots, was walking slowly. The dog ran with the speed of a stag; he entered like a lion, and fell on the enemy, who retired immediately into a secure corner. The Mastiff seized the cowardly assassin by the throat, dragged him to the door, and strangled him immediately.

Who can describe the terrible state of the mother's mind on her return? She saw the wolf stretched out dead on the floor; the Mastiff covered with blood, the bed torn to pieces, and no signs of the children. Having a presentiment of the terrible distress of his mistress, the dog moved towards her with energetic sympathy, then returning to the bed, he pushed his head several times under the mattress, seeming to say that she would find there what was most dear to her.

The frantic woman approached; she put out her hand trembling, and the innocent little children remained there without moving. She hastened to drag them out; it was high time; a moment later they would probably have been suffocated. As soon as they had recovered their senses, they described ingenuously the dangers from which they had been saved. The Mastiff, quite content with having saved the lives of the little boys, started to lick them, and gave them at least as many caresses as did their mother.

Another story from de Freville illustrates the immense courage and tenacity of the breed:

A Dutch merchant, who was travelling in Spain for the purpose of buying wool, had to pass through a forest in the neighborhood of Valladolid, which he had scarcely entered when a thief in ambush behind the trees called: "Stop, horseman, throw your purse into the hat which you see in the middle of the road, or if not you are a dead man."

The traveller, who had an excellent horse, and who was, besides, accompanied by Caesar, a very powerful Mastiff, well capable of defending him, had no thought of giving way to this threat and continued his journey without pause. He had not gone far when the report of a long carbine was heard. The bullet whistled through the air and the traveller, hit in the shoulder, fell to the ground.

The brigand, rich already in hopes, rushed forward to rob the Dutchman; but Caesar leaped at his throat and tore his face. Five other brigands then rushed out from among the trees, and forced the furious animal backwards with great blows of their swords, but he was not afraid of them and nothing could stop him. With his first rush he overthrew two of them and strangled them. A third mounted on horseback discharged a blunderbuss (Espingole) at the head of the dog, but missed him. Caesar made no mistake; he seized him by the thigh, and bit an enormous piece out of it, thereby forcing him to fall from his horse, and sparing him from a hanging. A fourth robber, who was armed with a big club, experienced a similar fate; and the two other rogues, witnesses of the skirmish, did not dare to continue the combat; they fled at full speed and went to hide themselves at the bottom of a well which had been dug in the forest.

After his victory, Caesar had no more pressing duty than to return to his master, who had been dangerously wounded; he was suffering terribly, and could not move, but was still full of life; he caressed his dog with a feeble hand and pointed his finger to the road which they had just traversed together and said: "To the inn, Caesar, I am lost." The dog understood this sign, and rushed immediately back to the hotel, which was about three miles from the place where the fight had taken place.

The dog's haggard air, and the wounds with which he was covered, caused violent suspicions in those who saw him enter. Everybody rushed out to see if the merchant was with him. Caesar came out again, and testified his joy. He rushed on barking, and when the bystanders followed him, he displayed even more joy. Eventually he acted as a guide, and conducted three well-armed men right into the forest.

There they found the unfortunate Dutchman bathed in his blood, and severely wounded. His horse was browsing peacefully near him. They lifted the wounded man onto a litter as quickly as possible, and removed him to safety. A skillful surgeon administered prompt assistance, and he got well in a few weeks, but he was deprived of the consolation of his faithful Mastiff, Caesar. The poor animal died the next day from blood poisoning from the terrible wounds he had received in the struggle. His last caress was for his master, who had placed his valiant defender near him in his own room, so that he might receive every attention.

The following incidents are extracted from Jesse's *Anecdotes of Dogs*, 1846.

A Mastiff belonging to a gentleman in Scotland, seeing a small dog that was following a cart from Kelso, carried down by the current of the Tweed, in spite of all his efforts to bear up against the current of the stream, after watching its motions for some time attentively, plunged voluntarily into the river, and seizing the wearied cur by the neck, brought it safely to land, in the presence of several spectators. . . .

An English gentleman, accompanied by a Mastiff, came to a place of public entertainment near Paris. The dog was refused admittance, and was consequently left to the care of someone outside. The gentleman soon after missed his watch, and went and requested permission to bring in his dog, who he said, would soon discover the thief. His request granted, his master made motions to the

dog expressive of what he had lost. The animal immediately ran about among the company, and traversed the gardens, till at last he laid hold of a man. The gentleman insisted that this person had got his watch, and on being searched, not only his watch, but six others were discovered in his pockets.

Captain Brown gives an interesting instance of the gentleness of a Mastiff towards a child. He says that a large and fierce Mastiff which had broken his chain, ran along a road near Bath, to the great terror and consternation of those whom he passed. When suddenly running by a most interesting boy, the child struck him with a stick, upon which the dog turned furiously upon his infant assailant. The little fellow, so far from being intimidated, ran up to him and flung his arms round the neck of the enraged animal, which instantly became appeased, and in return caressed the child. It is a well known fact that few dogs will bite a child, or even a young puppy. Captain Brown adds that he possesses a Mastiff which will not allow any one of his family to take a bone from him except his youngest child.

A chimney sweeper had ordered his dog, a half-bred Mastiff, to lie down on his soot bag, which he had placed inadvertently almost in the middle of a narrow street in the town of Southampton. A loaded coal-cart passing by, the driver desired the dog to move out of the way. On refusing to do so, the dog was scolded, then beaten, first gently, and afterwards with a smart application of the cart-whip, but all to no purpose. The fellow, with an oath, threatened to drive over the dog, and he did so, the faithful animal endeavoring to arrest the progress of the wheel by biting it. He thus allowed himself to be killed sooner than abandon his trust.

A carrier had a Mastiff remarkable for his sagacity. It happened unfortunately one day that one of the wagon horses trod accidentally upon him in the yard. The dog became furious, and would have attacked the horse had he not been prevented. It was usual for the dog to remain with the horses at night in the stable. After the men had retired, the mastiff selected the animal which had trod upon him, and, no doubt, would have put an end to his existence, had not the carters who were at hand, hearing an unusual noise, come to his assistance.

———————

The widow of a farmer had two Mastiffs, which, from their fierceness, rendered some precaution necessary in approaching the house. Their mistress was taken suddenly ill and died, and in the afternoon of her death, the benevolent wife of the clergyman of the parish called to see if she could render any assistance. After knocking in vain at the front door, she went to the back of the house in fear and trembling. On entering the kitchen, to her dismay she saw the two dogs on the hearth. They appeared, however, to be sensible of what had taken place, for they only lifted up their heads mournfully, looked at the intruder and resumed their former attitude.

———————

The son of a carter, who was studying at the College of Plessis under Louis XIII, had trained a strong Mastiff to carry his books, and to come for him at the end of his lessons. The punctual attendant, arriving once rather early, heard piercing cries. They were those of the student, whom his master was wishing to have whipped for a small fault.

The furious Mastiff threw himself at once on the hall porter and threatened to tear him to pieces because he offered resistance. He then rushed at the master who prudently fled, then dragged his young master away by the coat, and conducted him to his father's house without anyone daring to touch him.

———————

A Mastiff dog, which owed more to the bounty of a neighbor than to his master, was once locked, by mistake, in the well-stored pantry of his benefactor for a whole day, where there were milk, butter, bread and meat in abundance within his reach. When the servant returned to the pantry and saw the dog come out, and knowing the time he had been confined, she trembled for the devastation which her negligence must have occasioned. But on close examination, it was found that the honest creature had not tasted of anything, although on coming out, he fell on a bone that was given to him with all the voraciousness of hunger.

———————

On one of my visits to the delightful island of Bermuda, a friend, knowing my interest in Mastiffs, told me the following true story:

In the 1870's Colonel H. I. Wilkinson moved to the island from England, accompanied by his wife and a lovely big Mastiff. After a time it became necessary for the Colonel to return to England on business. Now, Mrs. Wilkinson had never cared for the Mastiff, for she was very jealous, believing that her husband loved the dog far more than he loved her.

After the Colonel sailed away, the wicked woman, in a fit of rage, had the Mastiff put to death. At his return, on learning what his wife had done, Colonel Wilkinson had a life-size statue made of his adored companion and had it placed in front of the window of Mrs. Wilkinson's room! From that day on, until her death, she was reminded of her evil deed—for which she was never forgiven.

———————

47

At left, Ch. Brompton Duchess (1915).

Above, Vereton Sir Titus (1915).

At left, Ch. Viscount (1915).

Chapter Eight

Great Kennels of the Past

Unfortunately it is not possible to mention all of the great kennels of the past in one comparatively brief chapter. It is, however, interesting to look back at some of the articles written by Mr. A. Croxton Smith and published in the magazine *Country Life* from 1914 through 1928, in which he discusses some of the great dogs and kennels on the British scene at that time.

In a 1914 issue of *Country Life*, Mr. Smith describes pictures of some of the famous winning Mastiffs of the time:

"Here we have photographs of some of the most typical Mastiffs of the present time; their owner is Lieutenant-Colonel Z. Walker of Fox Hollies Hall, near Birmingham. Today these kennels have to be reckoned with seriously whenever strong competition is afoot, Colonel Walker thus reaping the reward of many years patient striving. When he founded his kennels in 1875, he was up against a strong proposition, for during the next twenty years or so the dogs were at their best, many clever men were breeding them, and classes formed one of the chief attractions of leading shows.

"It may be that the beginning of the decadence set in with the advent of Crown Prince in 1880; his remarkably short head, compared with those of his predecessors and contemporaries, starting a fashion which, pushed to an absurd extreme, resulted in head properties being considered before all others, at the expense of soundness and movement.

"For close on forty years, Colonel Walker has been a steadfast adherent of the older stamp, his sole aim having been to retain as far as he could the correct type in all its purity. He has guarded his blood with the utmost zeal, rarely going outside his own establishment for his breeding stock, and if this became necessary, examining minutely the pedigrees of any animals brought in. He has absolutely ignored what he terms the pernicious practice of breeding solely for the show bench, or simply to conform to the fashion or caprice of the time being. To the eccentricities of fashion he attributes the deterioration of the true mastiff, for it cannot be denied that at present there are far too few good specimens in the country.

"Naturally Colonel Walker has bred many grand dogs. Of a long line one may recall Champion Stentor, whelped in 1888. Of the true type, he had a great skull, square muzzle, enormous bone and substance, combined with symmetry. He was a beautiful mover in all his paces and good over hurdles, nothwithstanding that in fair condition he weighed 196 pounds. In the last seven years he raised many noteworthy individuals and last but not least is Champion Charming Duchess, who won her full honours in 1913 at Birmingham, Cruft's and Richmond. They all have been beautifully sound and true movers although they have had great size.

"It is a pleasure to find one so enthusiastic about keeping up the correct type in a day noted for its abundance of dogs with the wrong expression. Colonel Walker was asked how he managed to get such substance on his dogs, to which he replied that he has no theories as to feeding beyond taking the precaution of seeing that the food is of a wholesome character and possesses a sufficient amount of nutritious properties. He adds that no amount of food, no matter of what nature, will alone produce size, which, like other characteristics, is inherited."

The following is adapted from an article by Mr. Smith in the May 8, 1915, issue of *Country Life:*

"One of the strongest kennels of the day is that owned by Mr. W. H. Shackleton of Keighley, who can boast of being the only owner of two living champions that have won all the cups offered, and are now barred from the Mastiff Club's 40-guinea cups, having won them five times. These notabilities are Champion Viscount of Lidgett, the brindle dog, and Champion Brompton Duchess, the fawn bitch. A dog puppy from these two, Vereton Sir Titus, is now advanced enough to justify one in speaking with some degree of confidence about his future.

"Mr. Shackleton is inclined to think that we have lost size in this breed. Adult dogs used to weigh anything from 165 lb. to 170 lb., and bitches between 130 lb. and 140 lb.

"The rate of growth is at its greatest between the third and the eighth month, which may be described as the critical period, during which malformations may appear, if the strength of the bones is not sufficient to bear the weight imposed upon them. Exercise needs much discretion also, enforced walking to the point of fatigue being distinctly injurious, but the puppies should have unlimited freedom in which to play about."

In the June 11, 1921, issue, Mr. Smith writes:

Above, Ch. Young Mary Bull (1921).

Above, Ch. Miss Bull (1921).

Above, Ch. Britain's Bell.
Below, Ch. Charming Duchess.

"At the beginning of the show era mastiffs fared very well, in common with others of the old breeds, and continued to progress as far as the last decade of the century, when a decline set in that became more pronounced as the present day was approached. In place of well filled classes at most of the important shows we have now sparse entries, half of which are so indifferent in character that their presence is a bad advertisement for the breed. The few that have any real pretensions to merit might almost be numbered on one's fingers. Among the best are those owned by Mr. R. A. Conquest of Castlemorton, Malvern, two being champions, viz., Young Mary Bull and Miss Bull, while the dog, Collyhurst Squire, has done a good deal of winning, being of a stamp to call for commendation. . . ."

In the issue of March 31, 1928, Mr. Smith says:

"A few years ago a man surprised me with his description of the wonderful collection of Mastiffs that he had seen at a local show in Derbyshire, the explanation being that Mr. R. H. Thomas, late of the Yosemite Valley, California, and Mr. C. R. Oliver had gone into partnership at Buxton. Since then the strain distinguished by the affix 'Menai' has become known everywhere. Ch. Yosemite Menai, apart from her successes in the show ring, has bred much good stock, which should be a corrective to a failing that has become all too common—loss of size. Her son, Anglesey Menai, is over 34 ins. at the shoulder, has a girth of 46 ins. and weighs upwards of 14 st. [196 lbs.] Juno Menai, a daughter, has great size for her sex. Mrs. Oliver, Winkenhurst, Hellingly, Sussex, has two extra good ones in Joseph of Studland and Joy of Wantley. Miss Bell, Earlywood Lodge, Ascot, had the honour of breeding Mrs. Evans's Ursula, which, although scarcely fully matured, ranks as one of our best bitches. As the Jersey exhibitor (Miss Bell) also owns Ch. Prince, the huge apricot-coloured fawn, it will be understood that she has quality if not quantity. At her first two shows in England, Ursula (Woden—Victoria Menai) won ten first prizes and two challenge certificates.

"Lancashire has a worthy representative in the first flight in Mr. Guy P. Greenwood's (Colne) Ch. Duke, a big dog standing on splendidly sound legs. This is an old strain, carried on by Mr. Greenwood from his father, who started it in 1877.

"The late Dr. J. Sidney Turner, who once owned a famous kennel, made some remarks in the *Kennel Encyclopaedia* that are as pertinent now as they were twenty years ago: 'There is no nobler looking dog, and but few nobler looking animals

Joseph of Studland.

Lady Here of Hellingly.

than a well-proportioned and active mastiff, but there are few more pitiable sights than a crippled giant. If mastiffs of the present day do not hold that high place in the mind of the public which they did in the "eighties" it is because the absurd craze for shorter and shorter heads has caused neglect of other characters so that the dog has degenerated into a monstrosity. There are still excellent specimens left, and if careful breeding was carried on, there is no reason why this noble breed of dog should not regain its former position.'

"One thing only should satisfy the ambitious breeder who is desirous of improving the race; that is, the 'altogether' that most nearly conforms to the ideal of the standard. It is the well balanced, symmetrical, typical dog that should win every time. We want a great head on a great body . . . we must be exacting in our criticism, refusing to have anything to do with mediocrity, and insisting upon size and soundness."

Huddersfield Kennels, owned by Mr. Norman Haigh, were established in 1922. Famous dogs at Huddersfield included Duke of Ashenhurst and Ch. Boadicea, who, when bred together, produced Cedric of Ashenhurst and Bernicea of Ashenhurst, both well known in their day. Another outstanding bitch at Huddersfield was Duchess of Ashenhurst, a sister to Duke.

Mrs. Evans' Ursula.

Grand Duke.

Ch. Boadicea.

Duke of Ashenhurst.

Cedric of Ashenhurst.

Havengore Kennels, owned by Mr. and Mrs. L. Scheerboom were established soon after Huddersfield began. Mr. and Mrs. Scheerboom purchased their first Mastiff, Crescent Rowena, in 1923, and continued to breed and exhibit Mastiffs for more than forty years.

When Crescent Rowena was mated to Ch. Master Beowulf, the first Havengore champion—Ch. Bill of Havengore, one of the outstanding Mastiffs of the day—was produced. And from then on Havengore continued to produce champions. Two of the best known were Ch. Mark of Havengore (Ch. Bill of Havengore ex Yosemite Menai) and Ch. Christopher of Havengore (Mark of Havengor ex Diane of Havengore).

When World War II began in 1939, there were about twenty Mastiffs at Havengore. Knowing there would soon be feeding problems, Mrs. Scheerboom dispersed her Mastiffs, keeping only three to serve as foundation stock when the war was over. Unfortunately, however, disaster overtook the two males, and the bitch Victoria of Havengore was unable to breed.

Gipsy of Havengore, dam of Rhinehart and Falcon of Blackroc.

Balint of Havengore, owned by Mr. and Mrs. Ivan Monostori, Oxford, England.

Drake of Havengore, Adam of Havengore, and Sammy of Havengore.

Above, Minting, Ch. Rodney of Havengore, Cathie of Havengore, and Samuel of Havengore.

Above, Hotspot of Havengore and Floria.

Above, Ch. Balint of Havengore with Mrs. I. Morostroni and Louise of Havengore with Mr. W. Hanson.

Below, Mrs. Scheerboom with Mastiff friends.

Below, Hotspot of Havengore and Gipsy of Havengore.

Throughout Great Britain the breed was much depleted after the war, and of the few Mastiffs which had survived, only a very small number were able to breed. With permission from the Kennel Club, the Old English Mastiff Club imported stock from the United States and Canada. Although the Club owned these Mastiffs, individual members undertook the care of the dogs —so Mrs. Scheerboom cared for Heatherbelle Stirling Silver—and the slow, hard work of rebuilding the breed began.

The first post-war Mastiff to gain the title was Ch. Rodney of Havengore (Valiant Diadem ex Nydia of Frithend). He was followed by Ch. Diane of Havengore (Hugh of Havengore ex O.E.M.C. Boadica) and many others—the most famous being Ch. Hotspot of Havengore (Meps Basil ex Flora of Havengore), who won many Challenge Certificates.

Between the end of World War II and 1965, when Mrs. Scheerboom stopped exhibiting, Havengore Kennels won about forty-five Challenge Certificates, and many Mastiffs bred at Havengore or sired by Havengore dogs, became champions.

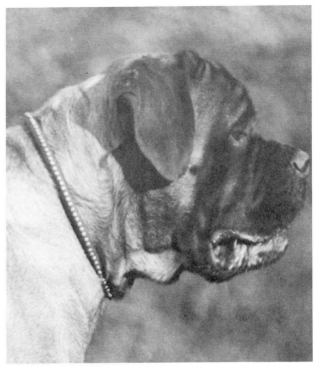

Ch. Christopher of Havengore.

Above, Mrs. Scheerboom's Ch. Bill of Havengore.

After Mr. Scheerboom's death in 1969, Mrs. Scheerboom was forced to move because of the local council's compulsory purchase order on her land. Although she disbanded her kennels entirely at that time, she kept two Mastiffs as companions and continued to serve as a Mastiff judge at shows.

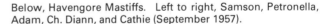

Below, Havengore Mastiffs. Left to right, Samson, Petronella, Adam, Ch. Diann, and Cathie (September 1957).

Above, Mrs. Mary Hector with some of her Mastiffs.

Above, Puppies at Hellingly Kennels.

Below, Comedienne of Broomcourt, owned by Mr. B. Bennett. A winning bitch at Crufts (1936).

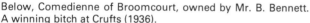

Mrs. Norah Dickin, whose kennel prefix was "Goring," joined the Old English Mastiff Club in the early twenties. She became Secretary of the Club in December 1933 and continued to serve in that office until February 1964, when she resigned.

A garden party was given for Mrs. Dickin at Lephan's Bridge Farm (home of Mr. and Mrs. Lloyd Jones) on May 22, 1965, and in appreciation for all she had done for the Club, Mrs. Dickin was presented with an engraved glass goblet subscribed for by members of the Club. (A photograph of the goblet is reproduced on the back cover of this book.)

In the effort to revitalize the breed in Great Britain following World War II, Mrs. Dickin had visited the United States and Canada in 1948 and 1949. She was also known here and in Great Britain for the chapter on Mastiffs she had authored for *The Book of Large Dogs* edited by A. F. L. Deeson. Her activity in the breed continued and she was serving as President of the O.E.M.C. for the 1966-67 term of office when she died.

Among noted kennels in Great Britain in prewar years were Hellingly, owned by Mrs. E. G. O. Oliver and mentioned in Mr. Smith's article of March 31, 1928; Broomcourt, owned by Mr. Bennet; and Tiddicar, owned by Mr. Cook.

Below, Mrs. E. G. Oliver with two of her famous Mastiffs.

Ch. Beta of Hellingly, brindle, winner of five Challenge Certificates.

Father and son. King and King Baldur of Hellingly. King Baldur was sired by Ch. Joseph.

Flora of Hellingly, a daughter of Ch. Joseph.

Ch. Britain's Belle.

Queen Bess of Hellingly, brindle, winner of a Challenge Certificate.

Headstudy of typical Mastiff dog.

Polly Gwynne.

Brian of Hellingly, a son of Ch. Joseph.

Ch. Joseph of Hellingly, patriarch of the kennel, winner of many prizes, and valued as a sire.

Cardinal of Hellingly, brother of Ch. Marksman and son of Queen Bess, and a winner of Challenge Certificates.

Ch. Ajax of Hellingly, one of the greatest Mastiffs of all time. Whelped in June 1929, he was bred by Mr. and Mrs. Oliver and owned by Mr. Leonard Crook, Blackpool, England.

Mrs. E. G. Oliver and Ch. Marksman of Hellingly, the first brindle to become a champion for some years.

Miss Oliver with three champions.

Elaine of Hellingly.

Mr. and Mrs. E. G. Oliver with some of their Mastiffs.

Ch. Joy of Wantley and Canute of Hellingly as a puppy.

Three Hellingly Champions: Ch. Duchess, Ch. Josephine, and Ch. Patricia.

Above, the imported Weyacres Lincoln.

Miss Ianthe Bell bought her first Mastiff, Squire's Daughter of Westcroft, in 1923. She mated her to Poor Joe, and a beautiful litter resulted. Miss Bell kept a dog, Woden, and a bitch, Thora, from this litter, and was persuaded to show them. Woden immediately gained awards and became a champion. From then on, Miss Bell bred many champions. Four of the most famous of her pre-war champions were Ch. Uther Penarvon (Rufus ex Bilichilde), Ch. Lady Turk (a brindle by Ch. Bill of Havengore ex Nerica), Ch. Ursula, and Ch. Hermia (a little sister to Ch. Lady Turk).

In 1931 Miss Bell moved from Ascot to Great Withybush, Cranleigh, and some time later registered the name of her kennels as Withybush.

Miss Bell had about seventeen Mastiffs in her kennels in 1938. Realizing that should war break out it would be impossible to feed so many large dogs, she stopped breeding and began to find homes in the country for her dogs. When war did break out, she kept three young Mastiffs (two of her best young bitches and a promising dog of eighteen months who had already done well in the show ring). During the war years, disaster overtook them, one by one, and the older Mastiffs given to friends also died, so Miss Bell was without a Mastiff for a time.

Miss Bell was one of the members of the Old English Mastiff Club involved in the revival of the breed following the war, and she took charge of two Club Mastiffs—the imported Heatherbell Portia of Goring (King Rufus of Parkhurst ex Heatherbelle Lady Hyacinth) and O.E.M.C. Pru-

Above, Ch. Withybush Crispin and Withybush Tauska with Miss Ianthe Bell.

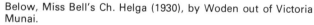

Below, Miss Bell's Ch. Helga (1930), by Woden out of Victoria Munai.

Below, first post-war breeding stock in England. O.E.M.C. Wolsey, O.E.M.C. Prudence, and O.E.M.C. Heatherbelle Portia of Goring.

dence (Valiant Diadem ex Nydia of Frithend).
The pedigrees of many of today's Mastiffs can be
traced back to these two bitches, one of whom
could be traced back to Miss Bell's pre-war Ch.
Uther Penarvon.

Miss Bell built up her kennel again and bred
many champions. Withybush Mastiffs went all
over the world, and the Withybush name is famous among all who are interested in the breed.
The best known of Miss Bell's post-war champions
were Ch. Withybush Aethelred (a magnificent
brindle dog by Weyacres Lincoln ex Withybush
Dusky Lady); Ch. Withybush Bess (Meps Jumbo of
Mansatta ex Jill of Flushdyke); and the latter's
daughter Ch. Withybush Fausta, sired by Ch.
Aethelred. Weyacres Lincoln (Withybush Magnus
ex Peachfarm Pricilla) was imported by Miss Bell.
Sired by a dog of her breeding exported to the
United States, Weyacres Lincoln is another of Miss
Bell's dogs to be found in a great many modern
pedigrees.

When Miss Bell died in 1960, there were again
about seventeen adult and puppy Mastiffs at
Withybush Kennels. Miss Bell left very firm and
clear instructions in her will that all Mastiffs over
two years of age in the kennels at the time of her
death were to be put down. This left only a few
young dogs of both sexes to carry on the line—a
sad loss to the breed. But Miss Bell felt it only
fair to her dogs, to whom she was devoted, that
they not be distressed by change to new ownership
and strange conditions.

Above, Hotspot of Havengore with Withybush Izod.

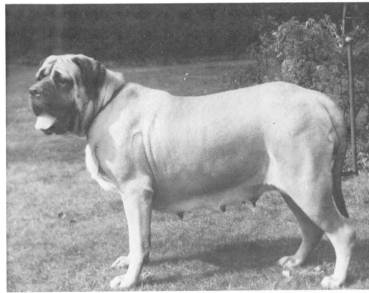

Above, Ch. Withybush Fausta, whelped December 2, 1957, by
Ch. Withybush Aethelred out of Ch. Withybush Bess.

Below, Ch. Withybush Aethelred, whelped 1955. Breeder-
owner, Miss Ianthe Bell.

Below, Ch. Baron of Moonsfield and Ch. Withybush Bess.

Left, Ch. Uther Penarvon, whelped January 10, 1929, by Rufus out of Bilichilde. Winner of four Challenge Certificates, nineteen Firsts, ten Challenge Cups, ten Specials, and other prizes at nine shows. Best Mastiff Dog at Richmond, 1935. Bred and owned by Miss Ianthe Bell.

Above, Withybush Beatrix, bred by Miss Ianthe Bell and owned by Mr. M. E. Perenoud, England.

Above, Ch. Woden, by Poor Joe out of Squire's Daughter of Westcroft (whelped 1924).

Left, Ch. Hady Turk, by Ch. Bill of Havengore ex Nerica. Winner of cup for Best Brindle for three consecutive years.

Above, Mr. H. Cook's Cleveland Premier.

Above, Ch. Tudor King of Lexander, owned by Mr. and Mrs. Anderson, England (1958).

Above, Prince Patrick of Penn, owned by Wardwell Jones (1930).

Above, Falcon of Blackroc, bred by William Hanson, and Mrs. Irene Creigh with one of her winning bitches.

Below, Ch. Vilna of Mansatta, owned by Mr. Fred Bowles, England.

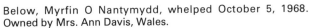

Below, Myrfin O Nantymydd, whelped October 5, 1968. Owned by Mrs. Ann Davis, Wales.

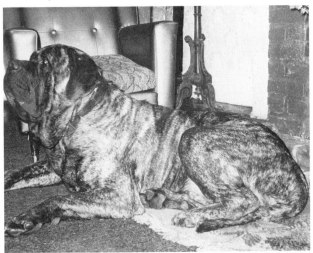

Copenore Centurion (1966).

Mr. and Mrs. Lindley of Copenore Kennels bred Mastiffs for twenty-three years, so the Copenore name is well known both in England and abroad. The kennel was started with one bitch, Cleo of Sparry (Faithful Gilliard of Sparry ex Malita Salome), and Copenore soon became known for strong, typical stock.

During her years as a breeder, Mrs. Lindley bred about two hundred puppies. Perhaps best known of her dogs was Jason of Copenore (Weyacres Lincoln ex Cleo of Sparry), who was whelped in 1957 and died in 1966. Jason did much for the breed—passing on his wonderful temperament, size, bone, and good head. He won the Old English Mastiff Club's Gold Cup three times and for six consecutive years he won the O.E.M.C. Progeny Award, which is given for the dog siring the greatest number of winners at championship shows during the year.

Mrs. Lindley's strong belief in line breeding is shown in the kennel records of fifteen champions

Ch. Copenore Mary Ellen at two and a half years of age. Sire, Ch. Weatherhill Bellringer. Dam, Pride of Taddington.

from Copenore. At one time Mrs. Lindley owned twelve Mastiffs which had won Challenge Certificates. Among well known Mastiffs from Copenore are: Ch. Weatherhill Bellringer (Jason of Copenore ex Ch. Weatherhill Milf Manetta); Copenore Centurion (a very black brindle by Withybush Superbus ex Copenore Prima Donna); Copenore Endeavour (Weatherhill Bellringer ex Copenore Prima Donna); Copenore Prima Donna (Jason of Copenore ex Withybush Kasia); Flourish of Copenore (Jason of Copenore ex Cleopatra of Saxondale); and Swedish Ch. Copenore Beauty.

Unfortunately, Ch. Copenore Mary Ellen had only a single litter, and it consisted of but two Mastiffs—Ch. Copenore Rab and Ch. Copenore Czarina—but these two became champions at the early ages of eighteen months and two years, respectively. They were later owned by Mrs. E. Degerdon, for Mrs. Lindley had to close Copenore Kennels in 1972, but Ch. Copenore Mary Ellen continued to live with her—a much-loved pet.

Cleo of Sparry, by Faithful Gilliard of Sparry out of Malita Salome. The first bitch owned by Copenore Kennels.

Endeavour of Copenore, by Weatherhill Bellringer out of Copenore Prima Donna.

Jason of Copenore at two and a half years of age. Sire, Weyacres Lincoln. Dam, Cleo of Sparry.

Caution's Own Daughter, owned by Mr. James W. Whitney, Rochester, New York. From an Artotype by E. Bierstadt, New York, in *Portraits of Dogs of the Day*.

Mr. E. H. Moore of Melrose, Massachusetts, was one of the earliest breeders of outstanding Mastiffs in the United States. He imported Ilford Caution (a son of Crown Prince), who sired the noted Ilford Chancellor. On the back of an early portrait of Ilford Chancellor (which is reproduced here) is the following:

"When Mr. E. H. Moore decided to give his undivided attention to breeding St. Bernards, it was a matter for congratulation that the best specimens of Mastiffs, which he had secured by wise selection and breeding, should come into the possession of such an enthusiastic fancier as Mr. James W. Whitney, of Rochester, New York.

"In Ilford Chancellor the Flour City Kennel has one of the best Mastiffs in the country. He was whelped on May 15th, 1885. His sire was Ilford Caution, one of the most noted stud Mastiffs of the day, and his dam was Brenda Secunda. He was bred by Mr. R. Cook of Ilford, England.

"After the sudden deaths of Champions Minting and Ilford Caution in 1889, and in consequence of Ilford Caution's great success as a sire, Mr. Moore, in the spring of 1890, imported his best son, the subject of this portrait, who had already sired winners in England.

"The dog had already made a splendid show record in England, also, winning, as a puppy, First at the Crystal Palace in 1886, and after numerous

First Prizes had been placed to his credit, he took the Challenge Prize at the Agricultural Hall, London, First at the Manchester show, and Equal Challenge at Liverpool in 1890. After his importation to this country, he was exhibited at Chicago, where he won First in the Open Class, and the week after repeated the victory at Rochester. In 1891 he was exhibited at most of the spring shows, winning First Prizes at New York, beating in the opinion of the judge, such a wonderfully good Mastiff as Beaufort; and wins at Baltimore, Pittsburgh, and Washington placed him in the Challenge Class, where he won at Boston, Chicago, and Cleveland.

"Ilford Chancellor is a handsomely formed animal with an excellent head of fashionable type, legs well off for bone, and a truly typical and well formed body."

Also reproduced here is a portrait of Caution's Own Daughter, another noted Mastiff owned by Mr. Moore. On the back of this portrait is the following:

"Caution's Own Daughter was whelped on May 5th, 1889, and was one of the last Mastiffs sired by the renowned Champion Ilford Caution, who

Ilford Caution. A print by T. Welch.

66

seemed to have the faculty of transmitting the main characteristics of his wonderful head. From Lady Dorothy, her dam, she gained that intense look of Mastiff quality, which is so much admired by connoisseurs of the breed. She was owned by Mr. E. H. Moore at his kennels at Melrose, Mass.

"When Mr. Moore dispersed his kennel of Mastiffs, he found a ready purchaser for his best dogs in Mr. James W. Whitney, of Rochester, N.Y. These formed the nucleus of a kennel of Mastiffs that could not be surpassed.

"Before she was two years old, Caution's Own Daughter made an excellent record at the shows held during the early spring of 1891. Making her debut at Elmira, N.Y., in January, she won First Prize. She was then shown at New York, where she took only Fourth in the Open Class, though she was entitled to First Place. In the Novice Class she easily defeated her competitors. At Baltimore, she beat her dam, Lady Dorothy, for premier honors. At Boston, Chicago, and Cleveland she again carried everything before her. She also won a large number of special prizes, including the Taunton Medal, at New York, for the best American-bred Mastiff under two years of age.

"As evidence of her intrinsic merit, she won these prizes notwithstanding the fact that she was, in a measure, handicapped by her chocolate face markings."

In 1932, Colonel Hobart Titus of West Roxbury, Boston, Massachusetts, scoured the country in an

June, owned by Colonel Hobart Titus, Weston, Massachusetts.

effort to find a pair of Mastiffs of correct quality and bloodlines. He failed, and learned that there apparently were only about thirty-five Mastiffs in the United States at that time. Then, after months of investigation, and with the help of English fanciers in making the selection, he was able to import the foundation stock of the Manthorne Mastiff Kennels. Goldhawk Elsie and Millfold Lass were the first to arrive. Both were shown and won many prizes before being retired to be used exclusively for breeding. They produced several very fine Mastiffs, one of the best being Captain Jinks of Manthorne.

Ilford Chancellor, owned by Mr. James W. Whitney, Rochester, New York. From an Artotype by E. Bierstadt, New York, in *Portraits of Dogs of the Day.*

Captain Jinks of Manthorne (1934). Breeder-owner, Colonel Hobart Titus, Weston, Massachusetts.

Left, Bursley Howland Titus with Goldhawk Elsie and Millfold Lass.

Below, Sioux Chief, by Ch. Cleveland Premier out of Goldhawk Jasmine.

Below (left to right), Manthorne Beauty, Manthorne Monarch, Millfold Lass, and Goldhawk Elsie. Owner, Colonel Hobart Titus, Manthorne Kennels, Boston, Massachusetts (1935).

Charles King, Jr., with one of the Mastiffs brought to Atlanta, Georgia, from England during World War II.

REFUGEE DOGS

With the advent of World War II in 1939, most of the kennels in England had to cut back on their breeding programs as explained earlier. This applied particularly to the large breeds, such as the Mastiff, but there were very few dogs being bred at all. The following excerpt from an article which appeared in the August 11, 1940, issue of *The Atlanta Journal Magazine* and which was written by Willard Neal, gives a revealing account of the Mastiff situation at that time:

"When German planes began to raid England, dogs were the worst sufferers. Thousands were humanely destroyed by their owners; others were put on short rations to conserve the nation's food supply. A blue-blooded few were shipped to the United States.

"Three of England's most aristocratic canine refugees came to Atlanta. An Afghan Hound found its way to the kennels of Mrs. Harold T. Patterson, 231 Peachtree Battle Avenue; and two enormous Mastiffs have been given a home by Mrs. Charles H. King, 439 Tuxedo Road.

"The two big Mastiffs [now owned by Mrs. King] barely escaped the war. [Due to the shortage of meat in England,] they had been living for months on a diet of vegetables and toast, with the result that each of them had lost about 50 pounds, so they tipped the scales at a mere 150 apiece—only about five or six times as much as an ordinary dog weighs.

"'I was lucky to get them,' said Mrs. King. 'I had written to the five principal Mastiff breeders in England to know if they had any dogs for sale. Four replied that they had done away with their kennels. The fifth, a Mr. Bowles, who lived near London, had put to sleep all but two of his finest pair of Mastiffs. They were named Remus and Prunella, and he shipped them to me.

"'About the time the dogs arrived, I received a letter from a famous dog show judge who suggested that I should try to find a Mastiff named Remus, the finest dog of its breed in the British Isles, he said. Since I already had Remus, his letter made me feel very happy.'

"The actual papers testifying to the aristocracy of the enormous refugees haven't arrived yet. Maybe they are on the ocean now—or possibly under it, if the ship bringing them happened to be torpedoed.

"However, the Mastiffs can speak for themselves, and they speak in a deep, throaty tone that befits their size and dignified bearing. They hardly ever bark, but when something really alarming comes up, their voices let a marauder know that he is being spoken to.

"Remus and Prunella are very dignified, and not afraid of anything from thunder to a 10-ton truck. When they first arrived they seemed terribly bored; they paid practically no attention to Mr. and Mrs. King. Then little Bonnie and Charlie King came into the yard and the dogs' eyes never left them. If the children walk along the fence, the dogs walk beside them inside the wire. There is only one thing Remus and Prunella like better than a romp with the kids.

"'They are wild about riding in the station wagon,' said Mrs. King. 'But we can take only one dog for a ride at a time. They are so big that one fills the car!

"'They are picking up weight rapidly, and I think they will weigh 200 pounds apiece in a few months. But I am afraid I have spoiled them. In England they had been on war rations, which means vegetables and cereal, and they were very thin and hungry looking. I started filling them up with three pounds of steak a day. And now they won't eat their vegetables!'"

Above, eighteenth century inkwell presented to The American Kennel Club in 1974.

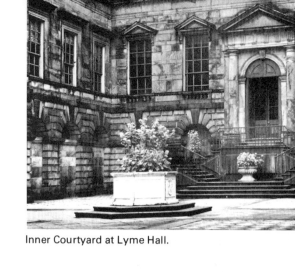

Inner Courtyard at Lyme Hall.

Above, Barry of Lyme Hall. Reproduction of a painting done by George Earle in 1870. Presented to The American Kennel Club in 1974 and may be seen at its offices in New York City.

Below, Main Entrance Gates at Lyme Hall.

Below, aerial view, showing West Front of Lyme Hall.

Chapter Nine

The Mastiff in Art

Many of the paintings and engravings mentioned in the histories of the breed may be seen at the castle situated in Lyme Park, Stockport, England. The magnificent castle was the home of the Legh family for six hundred years, and, as noted in earlier chapters, it is from the Legh family's famous Lyme Hall strains of Mastiffs, which date back over a period of more than five centuries, that today's English Mastiff has descended.

In 1946, Richard Legh, 3rd Lord Newton, presented the entire Lyme Park to the National Trust. In 1974, a sincere admirer of the breed decided that the castle would be the obvious place to put the many artifacts she had collected pertaining to the Mastiff. The National Trust accepted the gift, and two large rooms are being renovated to house the collection.

Pictured in this chapter are some of the Mastiff paintings and statuary that may be seen at Lyme Park.

Grey horse under saddle, with a Mastiff and a Newfoundland. Oil painting by Arthur Batt, 1881.

A Mastiff and a Great Dane embroiled in combat. Oil painting. Unsigned.

Miss Hale's Ch. Lion with "Dido" and Terrier "Nelly." Oil painting by Ignazio Spiridom, 1867.

"A Lion Hunt." Oil painting by DeVos, 1603.

"The Poacher." Oil painting by Richard Ansdell, 1868.

Oil painting by H. Hardy Simpson, 1882.

Mastiff, Terrier, and Pony. Oil painting by Ben Herring, 1855.

A child with a Mastiff. Oil painting by E. Wheeler. (Signed but not dated.)

Lady Flora Hastings. Watercolor by William Powell Frith, 1840.

Lord Lempster with Mastiff. Oil painting by Sir Peter Lely, 1685.

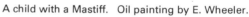

A child with a Mastiff. Oil painting by E. Wheeler.

Right, Two Mastiffs and a Toy Poodle. Oil painting by John Sutcliffe, 1820.

Left, "Monarch," oil painting by E. F. Holt, 1868. "Monarch's" name is on his collar. He is probably Wynn's Monarch, KCSB/ 2317, by Ch. King out of Wynn's Norah.

Right, "The Death of the Elk." Engraving by W. Ward.

Bronze by Barrye.

Bronze by Fratin.

Miniature, oil on enamel brooch,
three-quarters inch in diameter. W. B.
Ford, 1878.

Miniature, oil on enamel scarf-pin, nearly one inch in diameter.
T. E. Shaw, 1875.

Sterling silver decanter.   (Head is removable.)

Print by Sydenham Edwards (1800). From the *Cynographia Britannica.*

Oil painting by
Heywood, 1887.

Mr. J. Royle's distinguished champions of the show bench.
Saint Bernard, Spaniel, Mastiff, and Italian Greyhound.
Oil painting signed with monogram "SA," 1888.

"Ch. Meps Berenice." Oil painting by Smithson Broadhead, R.A., 1957.

Child in a landscape with Mastiff. Watercolor, unsigned.

Water jug with sterling silver top and spout, with Mastiff enamel affixed.

Cavalier standing in landscape with Mastiff. Watercolor by E. W. Andrews, 1876.

Vandyke's oil painting of the children of King Charles I with Mastiff. About 1632.

Mastiff and two children. Oil painting by C. T. Garland, 1883.

Mastiff in kennel with Terrier. Oil painting by R. S. Moseley, 1871.

Reclining Mastiff in a stall. Oil painting by C. Hunt, 1850.

The horse "Sultan," under saddle, and a Mastiff, two Terriers, and a goat in a box stall. Oil painting by Colin Graeme, 1881.

A Mastiff in a landscape with a Terrier at a hole. Oil painting. Early nineteenth century school of Ben Marshall.

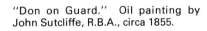

"Don on Guard." Oil painting by John Sutcliffe, R.B.A., circa 1855.

A cropped Mastiff and his kennel, with a Landseer Newfoundland. Oil painting by George Morland, 1792.

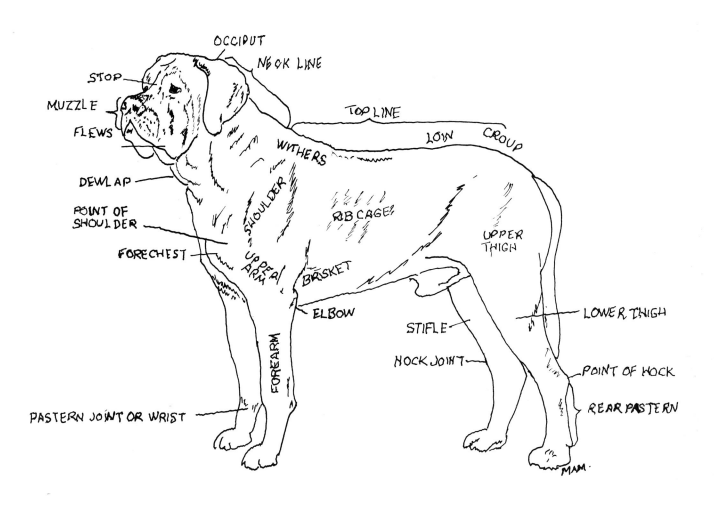

OCCIPUT

NECK LINE

STOP

MUZZLE

FLEWS

TOP LINE

WITHERS

LOIN

CROUP

DEWLAP

SHOULDER

RIB CAGE

POINT OF
SHOULDER

UPPER
THIGH

FORECHEST

UPPER
ARM

BRISKET

ELBOW

LOWER THIGH

STIFLE

HOCK JOINT

POINT OF HOCK

FOREARM

REAR PASTERN

PASTERN JOINT OR WRIST

MAM.

Chapter Ten

The Standard of the Mastiff

Every breed recognized by The American Kennel Club has an official written Standard which is drawn up by the national breed club and then approved by The American Kennel Club. The Standard is a description of the ideal dog of the breed and serves as a word pattern by which an owner may evaluate his own dog, and by which the individual dogs of the breed are judged at shows.

A Standard is not a document dictated arbitrarily by a small group of people. It is the result of the efforts and study of many breeders over a period of many years and is based on carefully kept breeding records and historical data.

As evolutionary changes take place in a breed, the Standard may be amended or rewritten entirely. But any changes that are made must be approved first by the members of the breed club and then by The American Kennel Club. These procedures prevent sudden, faddish, or inconsistent breeding goals from becoming paramount among breeders, for in breeding—as in exhibiting in the ring—the dogs must conform as closely as possible to the ideal expressed in the breed Standard.

The breed Standard which was approved following the Mastiff Club of America's incorporation in 1929, is no longer in effect. The current Standard of the Mastiff, which appears below, is a revision of the previous Standard, and was approved by The American Kennel Club on July 8, 1941.

The Mastiff Standard

General Character and Symmetry—Large, massive, symmetrical and well-knit frame. A combination of grandeur and good nature, courage and docility.

General Description of Head—In general outline giving a massive appearance when viewed from any angle. Breadth greatly to be desired.

Skull—Broad and somewhat rounded between the ears, forehead slightly curved, showing marked wrinkles which are particularly distinctive when at attention. Brows (superciliary ridges) moderately raised. Muscles of the temples well developed, those of the cheeks extremely powerful. Arch across the skull a flattened curve with a furrow up the center of the forehead. This extends from between the eyes to halfway up the skull.

Ears—Small, V-shaped, rounded at the tips. Leather moderately thin, set widely apart at the highest points on the side of the skull continuing the outline across the summit. They should lie close to the cheeks when in repose. Ears dark in color, the blacker the better, conforming to the color of the muzzle.

Eyes—Set wide apart, medium in size, never too prominent. Expression alert but kindly. The stop between the eyes well marked but not too abrupt. Color of eyes brown, the darker the better and showing no haw.

Face and Muzzle—Short, broad under the eyes and running nearly equal in width to the end of the nose. Truncated, i.e. blunt and cut off square, thus forming a right angle with the upper line of the face. Of great depth from the point of the nose to underjaw. Underjaw broad to the end and slightly rounded. Canine teeth healthy, powerful and wide apart. Scissors bite preferred but a moderately undershot jaw permissible providing the teeth are not visible when the mouth is closed. Lips diverging at obtuse angles with the septum and sufficiently pendulous so as to show a modified square profile. Nose broad and always dark in color, the blacker the better, with spread flat nostrils (not pointed or turned up) in profile. Muzzle dark in color, the blacker the better. Muzzle should be half the length of the skull, thus dividing the head into three parts—one for the foreface and two for the skull. In other words, the distance from tip of nose to stop is equal to one-half the distance between the stop and the occiput. Circumference of muzzle (measured midway between the eyes and nose) to that of the head (measured before the ears) as 3 is to 5.

Neck—Powerful and very muscular, slightly arched, and of medium length. The neck gradually increases in circumference as it approaches the shoulder. Neck moderately "dry" (not showing an excess of loose skin).

Chest and Flanks—Wide, deep, rounded and well let down between the forelegs, extending at least to the elbow. Forechest should be deep and well defined. Ribs extremely well rounded. False ribs deep and well set back. There should be a reasonable, but not exaggerated, cut-up.

Shoulder and Arm—Slightly sloping, heavy and muscular. No tendency to looseness of shoulders.

Forelegs and Feet—Legs straight, strong and set wide apart, heavy-boned. Elbows parallel to body. Feet heavy, round and compact with well-arched toes. Pasterns strong and bent only slightly. Black nails preferred.

Hind Legs—Hindquarters broad, wide and muscular. Second thighs well developed, hocks set back, wide apart and parallel when viewed from the rear.

Back and Loins—Back muscular, powerful and straight. Loins wide and muscular, slightly rounded over the rump.

Tail—Set on moderately high and reaching to the hocks or a little below. Wide at the root, tapering to the end, hanging straight in repose, forming a slight curve but never over the back when dog is in action.

Coat—Outer coat moderately coarse. Undercoat, dense, short and close lying.

Color—Apricot, silver fawn or dark fawn-brindle. Fawn-brindle should have fawn as a background color which should be completely covered with very dark stripes. In any case muzzle, ears and nose must be dark in color, the blacker the better, with similar color tone around the orbits, extending upwards between them.

Size—Dogs, minimum, 30 inches at the shoulder; bitches, minimum, 27½ inches at the shoulder.

Scale of Points

General character and symmetry	10	Chest and ribs	10
Height and substance	10	Forelegs and feet	10
Skull	10	Back, loins and flanks	10
Face and muzzle	12	Hind legs and feet	10
Ears	5	Tail	3
Eyes	5	Coat and color	5
		Total	100

Ethelbert at two and a half years. Owned by Mrs. Veazly, Mississippi.

Marlin at three months. Owned by Mrs. Monostori.

Deer Run Lancaster, Winners Dog at Westminster, 1977. Owners, Tobin Jackson and D. V. Gibbs.

Acadian Konigstiger, Best of Winners at 1977 Mastiff Club of America Specialty Show. By Ch. Acadian Bull Durham out of Renrock's Acadian Griselda. Owners, Rich and Marcia Benolken.

Deer Run Jericho City, Best of Breed. Bred and owned by D. V. Gibbs and T. Jackson.

Ch. Porky's Simba of Tingley, C.D., at Golden Gate Kennel Club Show, February 2, 1974.

Thunderhill's Cherub, Best of Breed at 1972 Long Island Kennel Club Show. Owner, Arthur Garutti, Jr. Breeder, Gary Wallace.

Ch. Greenbrier's Shambeau winning Best of Breed at the 1977 Westminster Kennel Club Show.

Dahlside Windsor's Bow Belle, Best of Winners at the 1977 Westminster Kennel Club Show. Bred by Mrs. Rodney Strong. Owned by Mrs. Lois Savage.

Gill's Bonnie Bell at March 1976 Harrisburg Show. Breeder, Clifford Graham. Owners, Sam and Marylyn Dollin.

Ch. National Ghengis, winning at 1970 Columbiana County Kennel Club Show. Owner, Henry Haynes.

Ch. Dahlside Dame Dickens, Best of Opposite Sex at 1971 Specialty Show. Breeder-owner, Mrs. Lois Savage. Judge, Mrs. Alice Seekins. Handler, Vic Capone.

Reveille Defender, Winners Dog, 1965 Mastiff Club of America Specialty Show. Owner, Mrs. James Syvertson. Judge, Mr. Stanley Dangerfield. Handler, Miss Damara Bolté.

Ch. Reveille Sentinel, Winners Bitch and Best of Opposite Sex at 1965 Mastiff Club of America Specialty Show. Owner, Miss Virginia Finley. Judge, Mr. Stanley Dangerfield. Handler, Miss Damara Bolté.

Hubert of Love Creek, Best of Breed at 1972 Orange Empire
Dog Club Show. Owned by Charles and Beatrice Kerr and
handled by Merry Wicker.

Mooreleigh Joyce, Best of Breed, Westminster Kennel Club
Show, 1963 and 1964. Breeder, Mooreleigh Kennels. Owner,
Mrs. Adelaide Bolté. Judge, Mr. A. B. Korbel. Handler, Miss
Damara Bolté.

High Hope of Skyhaven ("Julie"), Best of Opposite Sex and
Best of Winners at 1974 Santa Maria, California, Show. Owned
by Calvin W. Good, Jr., Fontana, California.

Mooreleigh Quentin, Best of Winners at 1968 Mastiff Club of
America Specialty Show. Owner-handler, Mrs. Marie A.
Moore.

Walnut Creeks Frederic Fonz, Winners Dog and Best of Winners, Mid-Kentucky Kennel Club Show, Hodgenville, Kentucky, September 1977.   Breeder, Mrs. Fred Bucknell, Jr. Owners, David and Sue Lulling.

Blackheath Boss, Winners Dog at 1971 Lafayette Show.   Owner, Mr. William Bibby.

Ch. Grand Duke O'Fem, Best of Breed at 1977 Old Dominion Kennel Club Show. Breeder-owner, Blanche Fontaine.

Warenhold Delilah, Winners Bitch and Best of Opposite Sex at 1971 Lafayette Show. Bred and owned by Mr. and Mrs. Robert Kross. Handled by Mr. Robert Kross.

Willowledge Mr. Chips, Best of Winners at the Mastiff Club of America Specialty Show, October 7, 1967. Handler, Mrs. Jane Forsythe. Judge, Mr. Peter Knoop.

Mooreleigh Joyce, Best of Opposite Sex at 1964 Mastiff Club of America Specialty Show. Owner, Mrs. Adelaide Bolté. Judge, Mr. Forrest Hall. Handler, Miss Damara Bolté.

Old Dominion Kennel Club Show, September 1968. English Ch. Tuppence of Blackroc (left) with handler Mr. William Hanson, and Ch. Goliath of Kisimu, owned by Mr. and Mrs. Peter Garr.

Ch. Bad Bascomb, Best of Breed at Olympia Dog Fanciers Association Show, October 14, 1973. Breeders-owners, Mr. and Mrs. Morris Hart.

Meps Berenice (left) and Ariadne of Sparry, winning at Mastiff Club of America Specialty Show, October 13, 1956, Catonsville, Maryland. Owner, Mooreleigh Kennels.

Ch. Cassandra of Cedar Hill, Best of Opposite Sex at Olympia Dog Fanciers Association Show, October 14, 1973. Breeder, David Cole. Owners, Robert Eby and Mary Lee Plumer.

"Mastiff Challenge Cup" presented by some of the members of the Old English Mastiff Club to the Mastiff Club of America in 1932.

Chapter Eleven

Mastiff Club of America Specialty Show Winners

To win Best of Breed at the Mastiff Club of America Specialty Show is probably the ultimate dream of every serious breeder and exhibitor of a Mastiff. Because there are more Mastiffs entered in the Specialty than in any other show held in the United States, competition is keen, and winning Best of Breed is considered the highest possible honor.

In June 1940 the Mastiff Club of America held the first Mastiff Specialty Show ever held in the United States. It took place in conjunction with the North Westchester Kennel Club Show at Katonah, New York.

In 1932 some of the members of the Old English Mastiff Club had presented to the Mastiff Club of America the "Mastiff Challenge Cup." Originally, the cup was placed in competition at the Westminster Kennel Club Show. Then at the Mastiff Club's annual meeting held in February 1940, it was resolved that the Mastiff Challenge Cup should be withdrawn from competition at the Westminster Show and should be placed in competition at such shows as the members of the Mastiff Club of America may designate at their annual meeting to be the Specialty Show for the breed for that year.

A perpetual trophy that cannot be won outright, the Challenge Cup is presented to the Specialty Best of Breed winner by the Club President, in the ring. Then the President keeps the Cup until the next Specialty.

Engraved on the cup are the names of Mastiff's which have won Best of Breed at all of the Specialty Shows held since 1940. No Specialties were held during the World War II years, nor were Specialty Shows held in 1954 and 1962. Listed below are the winners whose names are engraved on the cup for the years 1940 through 1977.

A true copy of winners taken from the *Mastiff Challenge Cup*—presented by The Old English Mastiff Club to the Mastiff Club of America in 1932:

1940	Aldwin of Altnacraig
1941	Boyce of Altnacraig
1949	George S. Strawbridge
1950	Agatha of Chaseway
1951	Peach Farm Katrina
1952	Peach Farm Hobo
1953	Heather of Knockrivoch
1955	Meps Bernice
1956	Adonis of Sparry
1957	Mooreleigh Moby Dick
1958	Adonis of Sparry
1959	Mooreleigh Moby Dick
1960	Adonis of Sparry
1961	Beowulf of Havengore
1963	Felton of Kisimu
1964	Rhinehart of Blackroc
1965	Ch. Rhinehart of Blackroc
1966	Windsors McTavish
1967	Ch. Reveille Juggernaut
1968	Ch. Reveille Juggernaut
1969	Ch. Ballyherugh's Cormac O'Conn
1970	Ch. Ballyherugh's Cormac O'Conn
1971	Ch. Reveille Defender
1971	(Fall) Rumblin Eko's His Majesty Thor
1972	Rumblin Eko's His Majesty Thor
1973	Ch. Rumblin Eko's His Majesty Thor
1974	Ch. Reveille's Big Thunder
1975	Ch. Reveille's Big Thunder
1976	Ch. Reveille's Big Thunder
1977	Ch. Greenbrier's Shambeau

Aldwin of Altnacraig, Best of Breed, Mastiff Club of America Specialty Show, 1940. By Duke of Hellingly out of Maud of Hellingly. Owned by Mr. James Foster Clark.

Boyce of Altnacraig, Best of Breed, Mastiff Club of America Specialty Show, 1941. By Duke of Hellingly out of Kathleen of Hellingly. Owned by Mr. James Foster Clark.

Peach Farm Katrina, Best of Breed, Mastiff Club of America Specialty Show, 1951. Left to right: Paul K. Hampshire, Baltimore, Maryland, President of Club; Mrs. John L. Brill, Newark, Delaware, breeder, owner, and handler of Katrina; and Charles Rhoads Williams, Philadelphia, Pennsylvania, judge of the event and founder of the Club.

Ch. Meps Berenice, Best of Breed, Mastiff Club of America Specialty Show, 1955. Breeder, Mr. M. E. Perenoud, England. Owner, Mrs. Marie A. Moore.

Heather of Knockrivoch, Best of Breed, Mastiff Club of America Specialty Show, 1953.

Mastiff Club of America Specialty Show, 1956. Left, Ch. Adonis of Sparry, Best of Breed in 1956, 1958, and 1960. Breeder, Mrs. E. C. Aberdeen, England. Handler, Mr. Johnny Davis. Right, Meps Berenice, Best of Opposite Sex, 1956. Breeder, Mr. M. E. Perenoud, England. Handler, Mr. R. Gordon Barton. Both dogs owned by Mooreleigh Kennels.

Ch. Mooreleigh Moby Dick, Best of Breed, Mastiff Club of America Specialty Shows, 1957 and 1959. Owner, Mrs. Florence Ewald.

Mastiff Club of America Specialty Show, 1963. Left, Felton of Kisimu, Best of Breed. Right, Mooreleigh Joyce, Best of Opposite Sex.

Rhinehart of Blackroc, Best of Breed, 1964 Mastiff Club of America Specialty Show. Owner, Mrs. Marie A. Moore.

Windsor's McTavish, Best of Breed, 1966 Mastiff Club of America Specialty Show. Owner, Marc Saunders. Breeder-handler, Charlotte Strong.

English and American Ch. Rhinehart of Blackroc (import). The first dual champion the breed has ever had. Best of Breed, 1965 Mastiff Club of America Specialty Show. Owner, Mrs. Marie A. Moore. Judge, Mr. Stanley Dangerfield.

Reveille Juggernaut, Best of Breed, Mastiff Club of America Specialty Show, 1967. Owner-handler, Mrs. James Syvertsen. Judge, Mr. Percy Roberts.

Ch. Ballyherugh's Cormac O'Con, Best of Breed, Mastiff Club of America Specialty Show, 1969 and 1970. Breeder, Gerald Danaker. Owner-handler, Gary Wallace.

Ch. Reveille Juggernaut, Best of Breed, Mastiff Club of America Specialty Show, 1968. Owner, Mrs. James Syvertsen. Handler, Miss Damara Bolté. Trophy presenter, Mr. John Brill.

Ch. Reveille Defender (eight years of age), Best of Breed, Mastiff Club of America Specialty Show, 1971. Owner-handler, Mrs. James Syvertsen. Trophy presenters, Mrs. John Brill and Dr. William Newman. Judge, Mrs. Seekins.

Ch. Rumblin Ekos His Majesty Thor, Best of Breed, Mastiff Club of America Specialty, 1971 (Fall) and 1972. Shown here at the age of seven winning the Veterans Class at the Mastiff Club of America Specialty Show, 1976.

Ch. Reveille Big Thunder, Best of Breed, Mastiff Club of America Specialty Show, 1974, 1975, and 1976. Bred by Mrs. Adelaide Bolté. Owned by Mrs. Robert Kessler.

Ch. Greenbrier's Shambeau, Best of Breed, Mastiff Club of America Specialty Show, 1977. Breeder, Mrs. Edward D. Funk. Owners, Shirley Lyons and John P. Smith. Handler, John P. Smith.

102

Chapter Twelve

Breeding, Whelping, and Care of the Mastiff Puppy

Almost every owner of a Mastiff bitch considers at some time the possibility of breeding her. The decision to breed a litter of Mastiffs (or a litter of any breed, for that matter) is not one to be made without careful study and thought. Far too many Mastiffs are bred carelessly, and far too many poor quality litters are produced. There is only one justifiable reason for breeding a dog, and that is to perpetuate consistently high quality in the breed. Unless the sire and dam are outstanding in conformation and temperament, giving the prospective breeder reason to believe their progeny will be of similar quality, the breeding should not take place.

Raising a litter involves many responsibilities. Training, grooming, conditioning—all are essential aspects of Mastiff ownership, and all should be considered seriously. It is hoped that the information that follows will help the Mastiff owner and prospective breeder to realize the responsibilities involved and thus benefit the Mastiffs of the future as well as those of the present.

Breeding

A Mastiff bitch will usually come into her first season when she is from nine to eleven months old. A bitch should not be bred at her first estrus, and, depending on her development, often it is better not to breed a Mastiff even at her second season.

The reproductive cycle is divided into four stages. The first stage, the pro-estrum (or "before estrum"), lasts about nine days and it is at this time during the cycle that the external genitalia are enlarged and the bloody discharge occurs. The second stage, estrum, also lasts about nine days and is the time during which ovulation occurs. Ovulation is the freeing of the eggs from the ovaries, and it usually occurs on the first or second day of the true estrus. However, the ova (or eggs) are not ready for fertilization until one or two days after ovulation. Because of this it is best to breed the bitch on the eleventh or twelfth day after the start of the pro-estrum. This is true of the average, but dogs are not all the same, so if you en-counter difficulty in getting your bitch in whelp, your veterinarian can make vaginal smears during the estral period to help determine the best day for breeding. The third stage, the post-estrum period, lasts about nine days, during which time the bitch is going out of season and, although still attractive to a male dog, she will not be receptive to his attentions. Then the bitch enters the fourth stage of the reproductive cycle, a period of about five or six months, after which she comes in season again and the cycle is repeated.

The gestation period is usually sixty-three days but does vary in some cases.

If the bitch is to be mated, the selection of the stud to be used is of great importance. In a breed where the choice is so limited, a very thorough study of pedigrees and bloodlines is imperative. A shy temperament is a very prevalent problem in the Mastiff breed, and the only way to work towards eliminating this unfortunate trait is to stop breeding shy dogs and bitches.

The owner of a Mastiff bitch should not breed her to a dog without seeing the dog first. No matter how big and beautiful the dog may be, if he is shy, he is not the dog to breed from. Temperament is at the top of the list as the most important attribute. Then comes soundness. Straight stifles, cowhocks, and splayed feet are a few of the defects which are known, for the most part, to be hereditary, and they must be avoided. Next in importance comes size. Height alone is not sufficient, for the Mastiff should have large bone, be deep through the body, and give the appearance of great solidity and power.

It should go without saying, of course, that you would not select a dog to breed to that has the same faults as your bitch. There is no such thing as the perfect dog, and, no matter how much you may love yours, it is folly to be blind to your dog's faults if you intend to raise better puppies and improve the breed.

It is important for you to accompany your bitch when she visits the stud. For a maiden bitch, it can be a rather terrifying experience and your presence would help her very much. After the mating has taken place, the dogs should be allowed to rest quietly.

All arrangements or contracts should be attended to before you breed your bitch. If a fee is to be charged, a clear contract, in writing, should be made between the dog owner and the bitch owner. It is fair for the owner of the stud to offer a re-service for the bitch in the event she does not conceive at the first service.

A bitch should be permitted only one litter a year. This practice leads to better puppies and a stronger, healthier bitch.

Every breeder should supply each puppy buyer with a five-generation pedigree. It does not matter if you do not intend to breed your dog—you might want to some day—and an extended pedigree is a must in preventing you from selecting bloodlines that would be incompatible to those of your dog. Pedigrees can also be obtained from The American Kennel Club, 51 Madison Avenue, New York, New York 10010.

Care of the Dam and Puppies

For the first four or five weeks of gestation, no special care of the bitch is necessary, and she should be encouraged to conduct herself as normally as possible. After the fifth week, strenuous exercise or excitement should be denied the bitch in whelp, although she should be given liberal exercise in the form of unhurried walks. The bitch should be tested and, if necessary, treated for worms no later than the third week. It is a better plan to worm her a week before she is to be bred.

One of the most valuable substances for the pregnant bitch is calcium phosphate, which should be added to the food daily in small quantities. Calcium and phosphorus are thus introduced into the system in a more concentrated form, and the ability of the bitch to produce puppies with sound bone will be increased.

In any of the large breeds, it is difficult to determine pregnancy by palpating the abdomen, but by the fiftieth day the milk glands should be enlarged and a few days prior to whelping the bitch will probably have some milk.

The amount of food for a pregnant bitch should not be greater than her usual intake unless she appears to be losing condition. It is a mistake to "stuff" your bitch, for excessive fat will not help the development of the puppies she is carrying and will only make the delivery more difficult for her.

Where the bitch is to whelp should have been determined at the very beginning of her pregnancy. It is best to have her close at hand so you can keep your eye on her at all times—and she will appreciate your companionship. A box at least six feet by six feet is needed, and it should be placed where the bitch is accustomed to sleep. Several thicknesses of newspapers make good bedding, for the newspapers can be changed easily and often.

When the first labor pains begin, the bitch will become restless. She will refuse any food and will start to tear up the paper to make her bed. There will be a slight discharge from the vulva and as the pains increase, the bitch should be watched closely. If the first puppy has not arrived in about an hour, the veterinarian should be called immediately.

After the puppy is born, the bitch immediately will break the sac with her teeth, sever the umbilical cord, and start to lick the puppy. If she is a young bitch and this is her first litter, she may not know how to do all these things, so it will be up to you to assist. The puppy must be removed from the sac as quickly as possible or it will smother. Then the cord must be cut with a pair of sterile scissors, about an inch from the puppy's body, and the puppy dried with a rather coarse bath towel. Be gentle but firm, for you want to get the puppy breathing normally as soon as you can. It is important to wipe the puppy's nose and mouth so the puppy will not inhale any fluid. Do not take the puppy away from the bitch. Keep it close to her where she can see what you are doing. Then place the puppy in front of her so she can lick it and be interested in it until her labor pains start again. The placenta, or "afterbirth," is usually eaten by the bitch.

The second puppy should put in its appearance about half an hour after the first one. If it doesn't, your veterinarian should be summoned quickly.

Generally it is quite easy to tell when the last puppy has arrived. The bitch will appear relaxed and quiet and she will take a greater interest in the family she has. The puppies should be nursing, and should be quite dry. They should also be kept warm. I have found that suspending an infrared lamp above the whelping box is the best way to keep the puppies in a temperature they like. Occasionally a bitch will sit on or in some other way smother some of the puppies, and I firmly believe it is because the new family was not kept warm enough.

Mastiff litters vary, naturally, in size. From five to eight seems to be about the average, but I do know of one bitch who produced fourteen and another who had one lone pup. I think five is the ideal number.

The puppies should be watched carefully to be sure they are receiving enough nourishment. If they cry a great deal and are restless, squirming around constantly, you may be sure they are hungry. In large litters it might be necessary to supplement the bitch's milk almost from the beginning. There are several wonderful products on the market today that eliminate the chore of mak-

ing up a formula that will agree with the puppies. The one I have used with the greatest success is "Esbilac," manufactured by the Borden Company. It is possible with the Mastiff breed to use a regular baby's nursing bottle, but use a sheep's nipple. In feeding puppies, great care in sterilizing all utensils must be observed as it is with human babies.

At three weeks of age, begin to feed the puppies solid food. Give them one teaspoonful of double-ground round steak with all the fat removed. They should have this treat once a day for a week, and it is amazing how quickly they get to know when dinner time arrives.

The next week increase the amount of steak to two teaspoons, one at night and one in the morning. The puppies are now four weeks old, so they should receive their first treatment for round-worms. Your veterinarian can recommend a product that is effective and easily administered. A powder which can be placed in the puppy's mouth and is instantly soluble is now available—a product that is nontoxic and does not require any previous fasting. A second treatment should be given two weeks later, after the puppies have been weaned. It might be wise also to have a fecal sample tested for hookworms, which do the most damage.

At five weeks a tiny amount of dry-type puppy food is added to the meat. The puppy chow, moistened with hot water and allowed to stand until it gets soft, should then be mixed with the meat and fed to the puppies in a dish.

Each puppy should be fed from his own dish. This is because some individuals eat faster than others and will, obviously, eat the food of the slower eating puppy if all the puppies are fed from one big pan. Also, when each puppy has his own dish, you know exactly the amount each pup is consuming and can increase or decrease the next meal to suit the needs of the individual.

The New Puppy

In raising any type of animal there are a few prime rules necessary for success. Common sense, good judgment, and keen observation are of major importance. Each puppy in a litter is an individual and his requirements vary according to his needs. No book can be written giving positive amounts and definite ingredients, like a cake recipe, so all I can do is to give the general basic needs of a puppy and leave the ultimate result to you.

If you are going to purchase a Mastiff puppy, it is best to get one that is from three to four months old. This particular breed is seriously plagued with shyness, and the personality factor does not usually become evident much before three months. If a puppy is going to be shy, he will start to withdraw from strangers at about that time. This trait is most unfortunate and every effort should be made to eliminate it. A shy dog is an unhappy, insecure dog and one that can, if cornered, be dangerous. Shyness is a form of fear, actually of mental imbalance, and it is definitely hereditary. So many people believe that the dog has been ill-treated, beaten, or otherwise abused, when they see one that is shy, but this is not generally the case. Dogs are born with this unfortunate trait.

Mastiffs become extremely devoted to the people who care for them, so the adjustment to a new home can be difficult when they are over four months old, because by that time they have formed a deep affection either for their owner, the kennelman or kennelmaid, or whoever has been their constant companion.

The decision as to whether to get a male or a female puppy is a purely personal one. Females, naturally, do not get as large as males, but in a breed as big as the Mastiff, this factor is of very little significance. Unless a purchaser is considering the possibility of raising some puppies, it is generally better to purchase a male. A female can be a considerable problem during her seasonal periods. Mastiffs do not adjust to new surroundings at all well as they mature, and therefore to whisk a bitch away to a boarding kennel or a veterinarian for her three-week stay is not the solution. If a purchaser really wants a bitch and has no idea of ever breeding her, it is wise to recommend having the dog spayed.

It is far more satisfactory to let a potential purchaser select his own puppy. It is also wise to let the purchaser see several adults before he decides to take a puppy into his home, for many people are not aware of the Mastiff's great size at maturity.

Regardless of whether a person has had dogs all his life and is familiar with the rearing of a young puppy, it is most important to have a detailed account written up for each puppy, giving the worming program that has been followed, the Distemper-Hepatitis-Leptospirosis protection, and any other medications or treatments that the puppy may have had. Also, the diet the puppy is receiving, the exact times of feeding, and suggestions of how much and when to increase the amounts, constitute important information which should be provided in writing.

Because of the tremendously rapid growth of a Mastiff puppy, it is imperative to give him the highest quality food and the quantity that he will consume readily. At birth a puppy will weigh a pound to a pound and a half, yet at three months of age he will weigh about sixty pounds.

Forcing the growth of a large breed puppy is highly undesirable, for it puts additional stress on a skeleton that all too often has problems holding itself together anyway. This is particularly true when the puppy is not receiving proper nutrition. An overabundance of minerals will be as harmful as an actual deficiency. Considering even the normal growth rates, the bone structure of the large breeds often develops weak spots—particularly in the joints. When this growth is further accelerated by adding minerals and vitamins to a balanced diet, more weight is accumulated. The stresses on the skelton are then more severe, with a likelihood of permanent problems resulting from lameness.

Breeders of integrity will provide feeding instructions to supply all the ingredients necessary for the dog's well-being throughout his life. Provided these instructions are adhered to, there is no need for additions according to personal fancy. Some puppies develop knobby joints at six to eight months of age and owners become alarmed. This condition is caused by a slight imbalance in the rate of growth of the radius, the bone on the inner side of the foreleg, but is one which will right itself in time. Unfortunately, a common reaction among owners is to supplement an already balanced diet with more calcium and vitamin D. Small overdoses of calcium rarely do much harm because the excess is eliminated by natural means, but vitamin D overdoses will seriously impair the normal condition by drawing the calcium from the bones into the bloodstream. If continued for long, overdoses will disrupt the ratio between calcium and phosphorus. Too much calcium and too little phosphorus will make bones brittle, whereas too much phosphorus and too little calcium will soften the bones.

The basic components of protein are amino acids. Of some twenty-two of these amino acids that may be available, ten to a dozen are essential to the dog. The high quality proteins contain these essential amino acids in desirable proportions. The lower quality proteins are higher in the unimportant amino acids, and may have few, or none, of the essential ones. A high quality dog food contains, among other things, complete protein in a highly digestible form.

Because signs of protein (amino acid) deficiency in a dog are seldom dramatic, it is easy to overlook their importance. However, the deficient dog eventually suffers from lowered resistance to infections and parasites, and loses skin and muscle tone, and in every case, aging processes are accelerated.

Mastiffs should be raised on a complete diet with nothing added to upset the balance so carefully arrived at by the dog food manufacturers. The Mastiff, ideally, should be kept on the slim side, rather than chubby, until full growth is attained and skeletal structures have had a chance to reach their maximum strength. A dog can then carry additional weight with greater safety, but weight bordering on obesity is hazardous at any age.

In addition to the medical history and diet instructions, every breeder should supply each purchaser with the individual registration certificate of the puppy.

Now that you have chosen your puppy, the time has come to take him home. Mastiffs are seldom bothered by car sickness, but it should go without saying that the puppy should not be fed for at least eight hours prior to his departure for his new home. It is a frightening experience for any puppy to have his security suddenly taken away and to find himself in a new and very large world among strangers. But with all the dignity for which the breed has been known all these centuries, the puppy will accept the new world and will ride quietly in the back seat of the car. After realizing that no harm will come to him, he will even enjoy the new experience and take an interest in the sights and sounds he has never seen or heard before.

On arriving at his new home, the puppy should be permitted to investigate his new domain by himself. He will walk around and finally select the spot where he wants to lie down and rest. He should be offered a drink of water and the bowl should be placed where he can find it easily, for Mastiffs consume a large amount of water.

After he has relaxed and rested, the puppy should be fed a small amount for his first meal. After he has finished eating, he should be taken out to relieve himself.

If it is at all possible, fix a sleeping place for the puppy in your own bedroom, and you will find that he will sleep quietly most of the night. A puppy does not like to be shut away somewhere all by himself for the night and, when in strange surroundings, will probably cry and whine all night.

A puppy desperately wants to be with people and will adjust rapidly to his new home when he is allowed to be part of the family.

Over a period of many years, the weights of three of the best bitches and three of the best dogs were compiled to determine the average weights at different points in the growth pattern:

Age	Bitch	Dog
1 month	13 pounds	15 pounds
2 months	28 pounds	36 pounds
3 months	42 pounds	60 pounds
4 months	55 pounds	81 pounds
5 months	77 pounds	108 pounds
6 months	89 pounds	128 pounds
7 months	101 pounds	135 pounds
8 months	110 pounds	158 pounds
9 months	114 pounds	166 pounds
10 months	122 pounds	170 pounds
11 months	130 pounds	175 pounds
12 months	140 pounds	180 pounds

The foregoing will vary, but the general trend should be constant for good, typical Mastiffs. The weight at two years will be a shade greater, but attention to diet and exercise is most important in order to combat obesity.

Training

Because of the puppy's great size, people are likely to lose sight of the fact that a Mastiff puppy is still a very young and undeveloped individual at six or eight months of age. His mental development does not keep pace with his physical growth and it is a mistake to try to train a Mastiff puppy before he is able to understand what is expected of him.

The first lessons to be learned are those which may be grouped under the general heading of "house training."

By nature the Mastiff is a very clean animal and housebreaking is virtually no problem. As with any puppy, a bowel movement will take place after eating so it is important to get the Mastiff puppy out of the house soon after he has finished his meal or had anything to drink. Also, after a puppy has been sleeping for some time and awakens, it is important to let him out to empty his bladder. Mistakes will and do occur, but the pup is so ashamed of making an error, no further punishment is necessary. The old method of rubbing a puppy's nose in his puddle and spanking him is an antiquated practice and should not be employed.

Since all puppies start teething at about four months of age, it is necessary to provide the Mastiff with his own chew toys, or the furniture will suffer. There are a number of excellent and harmless products on the market today that fill this requirement perfectly. Shoes seem to hold an enormous appeal to all puppies, so the new toys made of rawhide are an excellent substitute.

Generally speaking, the Mastiff puppy is unusually obedient from the very beginning, and will readily come when called, particularly if you make it pleasant for him to do so by making a fuss over him. Never, never call a puppy to you and then attempt to discipline him for some misdemeanor. If the puppy does not come when called, you should go to him and by a severe tone of voice correct him. Then walk away, slowly, and the puppy will follow. He should then be rewarded with praise and a caress. Immediate obedience is of the utmost importance, for then in any emergency the dog will always be under control.

Interestingly enough, a Mastiff does not have to be taught to "heel." A Mastiff instinctively walks alongside his master, with or without a leash. This is probably because of the protective role that Mastiffs have played for so many years. Also, the Mastiff learns quickly the meaning of the word "No" and will respect its use.

The Mastiff breed, as a whole, is intelligent, eager to please, possibly a little slow to understand something new, but willing and anxious to do whatever his owner may want.

If at all possible, it is best for the breeder to take the time to get the puppy acquainted with a collar and leash. Collars should not be left on the puppies while they are in the kennel because, in playing together, they can get hurt by having a foot caught in a collar, or having the collar catch on something. For a puppy, the best is a plain, round, leather collar. Choke collars, for the very young, are not good because young puppies seem to become quite frightened when the collar tightens.

If the first lessons are conducted more or less as a game, usually there is little trouble in lead-training a puppy. I like to take two puppies together, on quite long leads, and I let them wander around at will, only guiding them gently from time to time. After they become used to this, I then start guiding them more firmly and take them on trips up and down a rather long driveway. When they balk, as they will, I do not try to drag or force them, but wait until they make up their minds to get up and walk along nicely.

One of the first lessons a new Mastiff owner will learn is that it is impossible to MAKE a Mastiff do something he does not want to do. When a Mastiff rebels, he will lie down and go completely limp. Any attempt to put him back on his feet is to no avail. It is useless and, I might add, quite stupid to lose your temper with a balky puppy. There is nothing to gain, and in addition, your self respect and his confidence in you will suffer. Patience is the key word in teaching the young, and this is especially true with the Mastiff breed.

Overexercising a Mastiff puppy is a mistake. Because of his great weight, a Mastiff puppy is not physically able to go on long walks or chase balls or play "tag" for any length of time. The bones and the connecting joints are just too soft and unformed to carry the great weight without distress. If a puppy is forced to exercise more than he is able, lameness often results, which can be cured by rest. Allow the puppy to play at will, for he has sense enough to stop when he gets tired.

Grooming

To keep your Mastiff looking his very best at all times, it is important to brush him every day. Since the breed is relatively short coated—the hair is longer than that of the Boxer or Bulldog—extensive grooming is not necessary. However, Mastiffs do have a short, fine undercoat which they shed during the summer months, and it is important to remove this dead hair. To do this, it is best to use a brush with short bristles, which is called a "groom brush" and which fits in the palm of the hand.

The ears of all dogs should be checked regularly for an accumulation of wax, which is best removed by a veterinarian. You can assist matters, however, by making an inspection once or twice a week and dusting a small amount of powdered boric acid in the ears, for this is most beneficial in keeping the formation of wax to a minimum.

The nails of a dog should be kept trimmed so they do not touch the floor when the dog is standing normally. With black nails, it is difficult to see the quick, so it is necessary to take great care and trim just a little at a time. It is extremely painful for the dog if the quick is cut, and the nail will bleed. With white nails, the quick can be seen easily and the nail should be trimmed accordingly. If regular exercise is taken on any hard or rough surface, such as concrete or gravel, this will help to keep the nails in trim naturally.

A puppy's first teeth become loose at about the time a pup is four months of age, and it is advisable to watch for this to ensure that the first teeth drop out before the permanent set starts to grow in. Sometimes the second teeth will appear before the puppy teeth have come out, and then it is most important to have a veterinarian remove the first teeth so they will not interfere with growth of the second set.

Later in life, tarter is likely to form on the teeth, causing sore gums and, eventually, loss of teeth. Large knuckle or shin bones, which the dog can only gnaw at and not chew up or swallow, do help to keep teeth clean, but it is often necessary to have the deposits of tartar removed professionally.

To A Lately Imported and Very Distinguished English Mastiff

By George William Curtis (1824-1892)*

What are thou, noble beast, with ample brain
And face that beams with almost human thought;
With stalwart frame and lusty limbs that gain
Their strength and beauty from the days when
    fought
Thy far progenitors, among our English sires,
Or watched the night out by their camp-lit fires?

We draw thy lineage from the sea-girt land
From which we bring the virtues of our race:
Thy blood and ours have been in closest bond,
Through ages linked, with all unbroken trace,
Back to the hearths, the woods, the halls, the
    bowers,
When first began this wondrous love of thine for
    ours.

Some ancestors of thine, in centuries past
The Norman curfew heard and crouched to keep
Guard that 'til morn could all unhidden last
That Saxon households might in quiet sleep;
Or with the Barons' mighty league did stand,
In grim fidelity to win the Charter of the Land.

They kept the Northumbrian peasants ripening
    fields
Safe from the Scottish borderers' midnight raid;
They followed when Judea's desert yields
No slakening draught, no cooling noon-day shade,
When Richard from the Saracen strove to gain
The sepulchre of Him who on the cross was slain.

At home they roamed with Robin Hoods' brave
    crew,
To right the wrongs that cursed the Forest laws;
Again they rushed where'eer the bow-men drew
Their shafts in York's or Lancaster's fierce cause,
Or swelled the hosts that fought on Crispin's day,
And chased the flying French with deep-mouthed
    bay.

They joined the loyal shouts that rent the sky,
When the Great Queen rode down the embattled
    ranks,
And ope'd their throats, with heads uplifted high,
To roar defiance from the Kentish banks,
And leaped for joy to see the Northern wave
O'erwhelm the Armada in its watery grave.

In England's life, her story and her song,
Their faithful lines are now forever twined:
If baser uses have condemned to wrong,
Their blood, ennobled by the virtues gained
From ages of the good that Nature's law
Can from the higher brutes for man's protection
    draw.

Now thou art come, with all thy wealth of love,
To grace a home on this far Western shore:
And with ancestral pride for us to prove
Thy blood untainted and thy strong heart's core
Filled with the faith thy Maker gave to thee
That e'en in slavery makes thee bold and free.

Mysterious creature, in thy calm deep eyes,
We read as if a soul lay hidden there!
Is all thy nature, that we dearly prize,
To perish with thy form so grand and fair?
Say, shall th' Archangel's trumpet raise thy better
    part,
And prove that thou and me stand near the same
    Creator's heart?

New York
May 21, 1875.

    C.

*George William Curtis (1824-1892) was an American author, editor, and orator. His most popular book was a series of essays, *Prue and I* (1856). He was long one of the editors of the magazines *Harpers Monthly* and *Harpers Weekly*, campaigned against slavery and for civil service reform and woman suffrage, and was Chancellor of New York University after 1890.

Ruth's Answer to Mr. Curtis

By Samuel L. M. Barlow (1826-1889)

Why, pray tell me why am I deprived of speech,
So that answer to thy rhymed praise, is far beyond
   my reach?
Why, when the tale is told again of the glories of
   my race
My tongue is tied in silence and I speak but thro'
   my face?
Why my soul; if soul I have, as so plainly you
   premise
Must show its deep emotion thro' the sparkle of
   my eyes?

But I'll not complain—much less despair—I know
   that Nature's law
Was made by Him who made us both—is
   perfect—without flaw.
And if when this journey's over—and you reach
   the other shore,
I'm transformed into a molecule—and am nothing
   less or more
Than an undistinguished atom upon the pebbly
   strand
I'll e'en then confess His majesty and the justice of
   His hand!
And if prayers can then avail you (though this
   dogma goes for naught,
Throughout New England's borders, where
   Calvin's faith is taught.)
I say, if then, I still can prove my faithfulness and
   truth
I'll show my devotions, there's a Heaven on Earth
   for Ruth.

June 1875.

112